신흥교역국의 통관환경 연구

폴란드

한국조세재정연구원

2014년 11월 15일 1판 1쇄 인쇄
2014년 11월 15일 1판 1쇄 발행

지 은 이	세법연구센터 / 한국조세재정연구원
발 행 인	이헌숙
표　　지	김학용
발 행 처	생각쉼표 & 주)휴먼컬처아리랑
	서울특별시 영등포구 여의도동 45-13 코오롱포레스텔 309
전　　화	070) 8866 - 2220 FAX • 02) 784-4111
등 록 번 호	제 2009 - 000008호
등 록 일 자	2009년 12월 29일

www.휴먼컬처아리랑.kr
ISBN 979-11-5565-092-9

신흥교역국의 통관환경 연구

폴란드

한국조세재정연구원

※ 본 보고서는 폴란드 관세제도의 대부분을 담기 위해서 노력하였으나 지면의 부족 및 시간상의 제약으로 인해 부족한 부분이 있다.

또한 가급적 최신의 내용을 수록하기 위하여 노력하였지만, 사회·경제 상황에 따라 세제의 변화가 빈번하여, 가장 최신의 내용을 본 보고서에 반영하는 데에는 한계가 있었다.

따라서 본 보고서는 폴란드의 관세에 대한 최소한의 길라잡이임을 밝히며, 보다 정확하고 구체적인 사항은 폴란드 관세청과 재무부의 출판물 및 홈페이지와 관련 법령을 참조할 것을 권장한다. 특히 민감한 사안에 대하여는 반드시 관련 법령을 통해 확인할 필요가 있으며, 불명확한 부분에 대해서는 관련 관세전문가의 도움을 받을 것을 강조하고자 한다.

본 보고서의 내용은 저자들의 개인적인 의견이며, 한국조세연구원의 공식적인 견해와 무관함을 밝혀둔다.

목 차

Ⅰ. 개 관 · 9
  1. 일반 개황 · 9
  2. 경제 개황 · 11
      가. 폴란드의 주요 경제지표 · 11
      나. 폴란드의 수출입 동향 · 12
      다. 폴란드의 외국인 투자 동향 · 14
  3. 우리나라와 폴란드의 교역 관계 · 17
  4. 폴란드의 자유무역협정(FTA, Free Trade Agreement) 현황 · · · · · · · · · · · · · · 20
  5. 폴란드의 AEO 제도 · 23

Ⅱ. 외국의 통상환경 보고서 · 27
  1. World Bank의「Doing Business 2013」· 27
  2. 미국 국별 무역장벽 보고서(National Trade Estimate Report on Foreign
     Trade Barriers: NTE 보고서) · 29
      가. 비농산물 시장 접근성 · 30
      나. 농산물 시장 접근성 · 31
      다. 지적재산권의 보호 · 32
      라. 서비스 장벽 (금융서비스) · 33
      마. 세관 행정 · 33

Ⅲ. 폴란드의 통관 환경 · 34
  1. 통관행정 개요 · 34
      가. 통관행정 조직 · 34

나. 각종 수입 허가제도 ·· 38
　　다. 수입 제한 제도 ··· 44
　　라. 수출입 물품에 부과되는 내국세 ····························· 46
　　마. 관세의 감면·면제·유예제도 ································ 54
2. 수출국의 수입준비 (FTA 수출통관 준비 절차) ···················· 56
　　가. 품목 번호 및 관세 혜택 확인 ································ 56
　　나. 원산지 증명 ·· 57
3. 수입통관 절차 ··· 60
　　가. 물품 도착 전 준비 ·· 60
　　나. 물품의 반입 및 검사 ·· 62
　　다. 세금 납부 후 화물 출고 ······································· 63
　　라. 간이 절차(Simplified Procedure) ····························· 63
　　마. 수출 통관 절차 ·· 64
　　바. 관세 등의 환급 ·· 65

Ⅳ. 통관 절차별 고려 사항 ·· 67
1. 수입 신고 전 준비 ·· 68
　　가. 통관 절차상 특이사항 ··· 68
　　나. 애로 사례 ··· 69
　　다. 업무상 유의점 ··· 70
2. 수입 신고 및 세관 심사 ·· 72
　　가. 통관 절차상 특이사항 ··· 72
　　나. 애로 사례 ··· 73
　　다. 업무상 유의점 ··· 74
3. 세금 납부 및 물품 반출 ·· 74
　　가. 통관 절차상 특이사항 ··· 74
　　나. 애로 사례 ··· 75
　　다. 업무상 유의점 ··· 76

4. 수출 및 환급 ·· 76
   가. 통관 절차상 특이사항 ·· 76
   나. 애로 사례 ·· 77
   다. 업무상 유의점 ·· 78

참고문헌 ·· 79

부 록 ·· 81
   부록 Ⅰ. 비즈니스 팁 ··· 81
   부록 Ⅱ. 주요 유관 기관 정보 ··· 84
   부록 Ⅲ. EU Customs Code(EU 관세법) ································· 87
   부록 Ⅳ. SAD 서식 ··· 218
   부록 Ⅴ. EURO 1 Movement Certificate 서식 ······················· 219
   부록 Ⅵ. IE599 메세지 형식(세관발행 수출가능 메시지) ········· 220

표목차

〈표 Ⅰ-1〉 폴란드의 주요 경제 지표 ································· 12
〈표 Ⅰ-2〉 2011년 폴란드의 주요 수출 품목 ····················· 13
〈표 Ⅰ-3〉 2011년 폴란드의 국별 수출입 동향 ·················· 14
〈표 Ⅰ-4〉 폴란드의 해외 직접 투자(FDI) 유입 동향 ········· 15
〈표 Ⅰ-5〉 최근 우리나라의 對폴란드 투자 현황 ················ 16
〈표 Ⅰ-6〉 우리나라의 對폴란드 업종별 투자 현황 ············ 16
〈표 Ⅰ-7〉 최근 對폴란드 교역량 및 무역수지 ··················· 17
〈표 Ⅰ-8〉 최근 對폴란드 10대 수입 품목 ························· 18
〈표 Ⅰ-9〉 최근 對폴란드 10대 수출 품목 ························· 19
〈표 Ⅰ-10〉 2011년 우리나라의 10대 수출입 국가 순위 ······ 20
〈표 Ⅰ-11〉 한국 및 EU(폴란드)의 자유 무역 협정 현황 ···· 22
〈표 Ⅰ-12〉 우리나라의 MRA체결 현황 ···························· 26

〈표 Ⅱ-1〉 「Doing Business 2013」 폴란드의 무역 분야 순위 비교 ········ 28
〈표 Ⅱ-2〉 폴란드 수출입 소요 기간 및 비용 ····················· 28

〈표 Ⅲ-1〉 CE마킹 대상 품목 및 규정 지침 ······················ 43
〈표 Ⅲ-2〉 한·EU FTA 상품 양허 결과 ··························· 48
〈표 Ⅲ-3〉 한·EU FTA양허 단계별 주요 품목 ·················· 49
〈표 Ⅲ-4〉 물품 및 서비스별 부가세율 현황 ····················· 50
〈표 Ⅲ-5〉 EU 반덤핑 및 상계관세 규제 정보 ·················· 52
〈표 Ⅲ-6〉 원산지 증명 보관 서류 ···································· 59
〈표 Ⅲ-7〉 운송 수단에 따른 ENS 제출 시기 ···················· 61

〈표 Ⅳ-1〉 폴란드 통관 절차별 유의사항 ··· 67

그림목차

[그림 Ⅲ-1] 폴란드 관세행정 조직도 ··· 35

Ⅰ. 개 관

1. 일반 개황

□ 정식 국가 명칭은 폴란드공화국(The Republic of Poland)이며 2011년 기준으로 총 인구는 약 3,832만명임
  ○ 수도는 바르샤바(Warszawa)로 인구 170만명이 거주하며 주요 도시로 인구 74만명의 우치(Łódź), 76만명의 크라우프(Kraków), 63만명의 브로츠와프(Wrocław), 55만명의 포즈난(Poznań) 등이 있음

□ 폴란드의 국토 면적은 312,685㎢으로 남한의 1.4배이며, 유럽에서 8번째로 큰 면적을 가지고 있음
  ○ 국토 대부분이 북유럽 평야지대에 위치해 있어 지형이 대체로 완만하며 러시아, 리투아니아, 벨라루스, 우크라이나, 슬로바키아, 체코, 독일과 국경을 접하고 있음
  ○ 위치상으로 동·서유럽 중간에 위치하고 있어 발트해 연안인 폴란드 북쪽 국경을 통해 스칸디나비아와 북해 항구에도 쉽게 접근할 수 있음

□ 폴란드의 공식 언어는 폴란드어이고 민족 구성으로 폴란드인이 가장 많으며 약 90%의 국민이 가톨릭을 신봉함
  ○ 가톨릭교를 제외하고 신교, 러시아 정교 등이 10%를 차지하고 있음
  ○ 민족은 폴란드인(97%)과 기타 독일인, 벨라루스인, 우크라이나인(3%)으로 구성됨

□ 국가 형태는 공화국이고 정부 형태는 대통령제가 가미된 의원내각제로서 임기 4년의 양원제 의회를 채택하고 있음
  ○ 대통령이 하원 다수당과 협의하여 총리를 지명하면 총리 지명자는 내각을 구성

한 후 대통령의 임명과 하원의 인준을 받음
- ○ 총리는 하원에만 책임을 지며, 대통령은 총리 해임권이 없음
- ○ 현재 주요 정당은 시민연단(PO), 법과 정의당(PiS), 팔리코트지지운동(RP) 등임

□ 폴란드는 1989년 체제전환 후 급진적 경제개혁을 실시하여 공산주의 경제에서 자본주의로의 전환에 성공한 경제모델임
- ○ 공산권 붕괴 후 동유럽 국가 중 가장 빠른 성장(1990년대 연평균 6% 경제성장)을 달성함
- ○ 높은 경제성장을 바탕으로 1996년 우리나라와 함께 경제협력개발기구(OECD)에 가입하였으며 2004년 유럽연합(EU)의 회원국이 됨

□ 과거 전통적 농업국가였으나 공산 정권하에서 공업화에 주력하여 기계, 중화학 공업 등이 발전하며 산업 기반이 구축됨

□ 현재는 서비스업이 전체 산업의 절반가량을 차지하는 선진국형 산업구조를 가지고 있으며, 자동차, IT, 전기전자, 항공, 기계 등의 부문이 중점적으로 육성되고 있음
- ○ 특히 폴란드는 중동부 유럽지역에서 중요한 자동차 생산기지이며 GM, 폭스바겐, 피아트 등의 유명 자동차 기업들이 폴란드에 진출해 있음

□ 폴란드의 화폐 단위는 즈워티(Złoty)이며 2011년 기준으로 미국 1달러(Dollar)는 4.12즈워티이고 1유로(Euro)는 12.4즈워티임

□ 폴란드는 상당한 광물자원과 농업자원을 보유하고 있으며 이러한 천연자원은 폴란드의 수출에 크게 기여하고 있음
- ○ 폴란드는 무연탄과 갈탄의 세계 5위 보유국이며 이 밖에도 구리, 황, 아연, 납, 은, 마그네슘, 암염 등의 광물자원 보유국임
- ○ 폴란드의 주요 농산물은 밀, 감자, 사탕무, 사료용 작물 등이며 1천 870만헥타르의 토지가 경작 가능하고 890만헥타르의 토지는 방목과 임업에 사용됨

I. 개 관 11

□ 폴란드는 1948년 북한과도 외교 관계를 수립하였으며 북한과의 총교역규모는 2007년 폴란드를 기준으로 1,773만달러임

2. 경제 개황

가. 폴란드의 주요 경제지표

□ 국제적인 경제 불안에도 불구하고 2011년 4.3%의 경제성장을 달성하였으며 건설 및 인프라 분야의 활발한 투자와 EU역내 수출 증대가 경제성장의 주요 원인으로 꼽힘
  ○ 이는 EU국가 27개국 평균 경제성장률(1.6%) 보다 두 배 이상 높은 수치임

□ 건설업은 2009년 상업용 건물 및 개인주택 건설 감소로 침체를 보여 왔으나 2010년 EU펀드의 조기 집행과 '유로 2012' 관련 인프라 건설을 확대하며 회복세로 반전됨

□ 폴란드 즈워티화(貨)는 미국 재정수지 악화 및 신용 등급 하락, 그리스발 신용 위기로 인한 국제 환율 시장의 변동으로 약세로 전환됨

□ 폴란드 재정적자는 2009년과 2010년 각각 GDP 대비 7.2%와 7.9%를 기록하여 2011년 초 EU집행위의 경고를 받은 바 있음
  ○ 폴란드 정부는 2010년 3월 재정적자 감소를 위해 연금개혁 및 공기업 민영화 등의 노력을 기울여 왔으며 2011년 재정적자는 약 5% 정도로 추정하고 있음

□ 폴란드 정부는 2012년까지 재정적자를 2.9%로 낮추는 것을 목표로 하고 있음

□ 2008년 말부터 이슈가 되어온 폴란드의 유로화 도입은 정부 재정수지 증가 및 그리스 등 남유럽으로부터 촉발된 유럽 금융위기로 인해 목표시한이 2015년으로 미뤄짐

〈표 Ⅰ-1〉 폴란드의 주요 경제 지표

구분	2007	2008	2009	2010	2011*
명목 GDP(억달러)	4,251	5,294	4,305	4,692	5,135
경제성장률(%)	6.8	5.1	1.6	3.9	4.3
1인당 GDP(달러)	16,360	17,580*	18,025*	18,923*	20,169
물가상승률(%)	2.5	4.2	3.5	2.6	3.9
실업률(%)	12.7	9.8	11.0	12.1	12.4
환율(Zloty/달러)	2.77	2.41	3.12	3.02	2.96
환율(Zloty/유로)	3.78	3.52	4.33	3.99	4.12
수출(억달러)	1,378	1,695	1,336	1,557	1,889.5
수입(억달러)	1,619	2,060	1,457	1,736	2,094.0
정부재정적자폭**	-1.9	-3.7	-7.3	-7.8	-5.1

주: *는 추정치 **는 GDP 대비 %
자료: Economist Intelligence Unit, Country report 2012, 중앙은행(NBP), 폴란드 통계청(GUS)

나. 폴란드의 수출입 동향

□ 폴란드의 2011년 수출은 전년 대비 미화 기준 약 21% 증가한 1,889억달러를 기록하였으며 수입은 약 20%가 증가한 2,078억달러를 기록함

□ 유럽 경제위기 속에서도 수출이 증가한 배경은 유로화 대비 폴란드 즈워티화(貨)의 약세로 인한 폴란드 제품의 수요 증가로 추정됨

□ 반면 즈워티화의 약세로 인해 원유 및 국제 원자재 가격상승이 수입에 부담으로 작용하며 무역 적자액은 2010년보다 약 11% 상승한 203억달러 가량을 기록함

□ 폴란드의 주요 수출품은 운송수단, 기계, 가구 및 침구류 등이며, 주요 수입 품목으로는 광물 및 석유 연료, 기계, 운송수단, 플라스틱 등이 있음

□ 수출품의 상위를 차지하고 있는 운송수단 중 자동차의 경우 2010년 제조업의 약 11%를 차지하고 있으며 2011년 승용차 생산량 기준으로 약 85만대의 규모를 가지고 있음

□ 광물 및 석유 연료와 철강 제품의 수출입이 두드러진 성장세를 나타내고 있으며 전기기계류에서 수출입 둔화를 관찰할 수 있음

〈표 Ⅰ-2〉 2011년 폴란드의 주요 수출 품목

(단위: 백만달러)

수출				수입			
품목	2009	2010	2011	품목	2009	2010	2011
운송수단 (기차 제외)	20,296.55	20,790.49	23,800.39	광물연료, 석유 등	14,169.33	19,115.32	26,546.23
기계	17,709.38	20,486.97	23,034.50	기계	20,533.45	22,173.02	24,818.46
전기기계	17,620.84	21,194.01	21,162.03	전기기계	17,671.44	21,335.38	20,724.93
가구 및 침구류	7,743.40	8,555.73	9,943.33	운송수단 (기차 제외)	12,442.70	14,716.48	16,769.02
광물연료, 석유 등	4,228.32	6,558.46	9,225.76	플라스틱	8,204.08	9,995.98	11,948.46
플라스틱	5,406.35	6,655.46	8,179.49	철 및 강철제품	5,002.39	6,627.16	8,462.64
철 및 강철제품	4,800.84	5,133.47	6,469.14	광학용품	4,711.71	5,490.03	6,036.40
철 및 강철	2,845.44	3,826.54	5,365.93	의료재	5,024.65	5,727.06	6,004.18
고무	2,907.93	3,776.25	5,044.49	철 및 강철	3,950.47	4,237.22	5,223.93
배 및 선박	3,489.97	3,231.56	5,006.03	기타	3,447.98	3,760.09	5,038.87

자료: World Trade Atlas, 한국무역협회(KITA)

□ 폴란드 전체 무역에서 독일이 차지하는 비중이 가장 높으며 독일은 2011년 전체 수출의 26.1%, 전체 수입의 27.62%를 차지하는 것으로 나타남

□ EU국가들을 상대로 한 교역이 폴란드 전체 무역의 60% 이상을 차지하며 러시아를

EU 교역상대로 포함시키는 경우 폴란드 전체 무역의 EU 국가 의존도가 70~80%에 달함

〈표 Ⅰ-3〉 2011년 폴란드의 국별 수출입 동향

(단위: 백만달러)

순위	수 출		수 입	
	국가명	금액	국가명	금액
1	독일	48,890.91	독일	57,403.42
2	영국	12,034.41	러시아	25,163.77
3	체코공화국	11,627.02	네덜란드	11,757.59
4	프랑스	11,481.74	이탈리아	10,685.25
5	이탈리아	10,056.27	중국	10,607.89
6	러시아	8,448.09	프랑스	8,810.69
7	네덜란드	8,173.89	체코공화국	8,542.22
8	스웨덴	5,336.51	벨기에	6,416.66
9	헝가리	4,793.07	영국	5,726.13
10	우크라이나	4,665.97	슬로바키아	5,089.67

자료: World Trade Atlas

다. 폴란드의 외국인 투자 동향

□ 1989년 폴란드의 시장경제체제 전환을 계기로 1990년대 초반부터 서유럽 기업들을 중심으로 외국인 투자 진출이 시작됨
  ○ 2007년 말에는 외국인 직접투자(FDI) 유입 누적액이 1천억유로를 넘어서며 중동부 유럽국가 중 헝가리 다음으로 많은 투자를 유치한 국가가 됨[1]

□ 2008년 경제위기의 여파로 감소세로 돌아섰던 폴란드 내 외국인 투자 유입액은 2011년 다시 성장세로 돌아서서 3분기 말 기준으로 누적액 90억유로를 기록함

---

1) KBC 바르샤바 무역관

□ 폴란드 투자청(PAIiIZ)에 따르면 2011년 말 기준으로 외국인 투자가 활발한 분야는 자동차, 비즈니스 프로세스 아웃소싱, 기계 산업, 전자 산업 및 ICT 분야임

□ 폴란드의 전체 외국인 투자 중 85%를 EU국가가 차지하고 있으며 유럽 외 국가로 미국, 아시아 국가에서 2009년 기준으로 일본과 우리나라가 각각 1, 2위를 차지하고 있음

□ 국제연합무역개발협의회(UNCTAD)의 2011년 세계투자보고서(World Investment Report)에 따르면 다국적 기업들은 향후 3년간 주요 투자처로 폴란드를 6위로 지목함
  ○ 유럽 내 경제위기에도 폴란드 투자에 대한 국제적인 시각은 우호적인 것을 알 수 있음

〈표 I-4〉 폴란드의 해외 직접 투자(FDI) 유입 동향

(단위: 백만달러)

연도	2007	2008	2009	2010	2011*
투자유입액	17,242	10,085	9,863	6,686	9,000

주: * 2011년은 3분기까지 수치
자료: 폴란드 중앙은행(NBP)

□ 우리나라의 對폴란드 투자는 2008년 세계 금융위기 이후 큰 폭으로 감소하였으나 2011년에 들어와서 신고 금액과 투자 금액이 약 두 배가량 증가하고 있음

□ 2011년 말 기준으로 우리나라의 對폴란드 해외 직접 투자 누적액은 약 12억 9,600만 달러로 우리나라의 對EU 투자 중 5위를 기록함
  ○ 한국의 對EU 투자 순위는 영국(88.3억달러), 네덜란드(62.6억달러), 독일(36억달러), 아일랜드(14.8억달러), 폴란드(12.9억달러) 순서임[2)]

---

2) 한국수출입은행, 한국무역협회(KITA)

<표 Ⅰ-5> 최근 우리나라의 對폴란드 투자 현황

(단위: 건, 개, 천달러)

	신고건수	신규법인 수	신고금액	송금횟수	투자금액
2008년	40	12	105,412	63	93,430
2009년	8	1	28,770	19	28,939
2010년	23	8	37,291	23	28,640
2011년	21	5	59,603	25	42,191

주: 법인은 현지 법인을 대상으로 함
자료: 한국수출입은행 해외투자통계

□ 1990년대 중반부터 시작된 우리기업의 폴란드 투자는 제조업 중심의 생산설비 투자이며 자동차, 가전 분야가 주를 이루고 있음
  ○ 2011년 역시 제조업 중심으로 투자가 이루어지고 있으며 금액 기준으로 제조업이 전체 투자의 90%를 차지하고 있음

□ 2011년에 들어와서 우리나라는 폴란드의 보건 및 사회 복지 서비스업에 새롭게 투자를 시작함
  ○ 반면 도·소매업의 투자금액은 현저히 줄어들었으며 운수업의 투자 금액 또한 줄어들고 있음

<표 Ⅰ-6> 우리나라의 對폴란드 업종별 투자 현황

(단위: 천달러, 건)

2010 순위	투자 업종	2010년		2011년	
		투자금액	신고건수	투자금액	신고건수
1	제조업	28,490	16	41,856	15
2	건설업	17	1	192	1
3	도매 및 소매업	71	4	0	0
4	운수업	62	2	36	3
5	보건업 및 사회복지 서비스업	-	-	107	2

주: 법인은 현지 법인을 대상으로 함
자료: 한국수출입은행 해외투자통계

□ 제조업에 대한 우리 기업의 투자는 바르샤바 근교, 독일 국경과 가까운 브로츠와프 지역 및 카토비체 지역에 집중되고 있음
  ○ 특히 브로츠와프는 우리 전자 기업이 가장 많이 투자한 지역으로서 LCD 패널 및 LCD TV 생산업체들이 진출해 있으며 카토비체 지역은 자동차 부품업체들이 진출해 있음

3. 우리나라와 폴란드의 교역 관계

□ 폴란드는 우리나라의 전통적인 무역수지 흑자 대상국으로서 2010년까지 흑자 폭이 지속적으로 증가하여 EU 국가 내 수출 5위, 무역수지 2위를 기록함

□ 2011년 우리나라의 對폴란드 수출은 6.4% 감소하였으나 수입은 37.4% 증가함
  ○ 유럽 경제위기로 인한 폴란드 내 한국 투자기업의 생산 부자재 수입 감소가 중요한 요인이라고 볼 수 있음

〈표 I-7〉 최근 對폴란드 교역량 및 무역수지

(단위: 백만달러, %)

구분	2007	2008	2009	2010	2011
수출 (전년 대비 증감률)	35.1(34.3)	41.1(17.3)	41.5(0.7)	43.8(5.6)	41.0(-6.4)
수입 (전년 대비 증감률)	3.0(11.2)	3.1(2.0)	2.3(-23.9)	2.7(17.1)	3.8(37.4)
무역수지	32.1	38.1	39.1	41.1	37.2

자료: 한국무역협회(KITA)

□ 수출 감소 및 수입 증가에도 불구하고 對폴란드 수출은 EU 국가 내 수출 순위에서 5위인 이탈리아와 약 700만달러 차이로 7위를 차지하며 무역수지 흑자 규모로는 EU 국가 중 2위를 기록함[3]

□ 특히 2010년에 비해 2011년의 한국 對폴란드 수입은 3배가량 증가하였으며 이는 원동기 및 펌프, 육류, 유리제품 수입의 급증에 기인함

□ 우리나라의 2011년 對폴란드 주요 수입품은 원동기 및 펌프, 육류, 타일 및 도자기 제품, 자동차 부품, 운반 하역 기계 등이며 2010년과 비교하여 건설광산기계, 계측제어분석기 등의 수입이 감소함

〈표 Ⅰ-8〉 최근 對폴란드 10대 수입 품목

(단위: 천달러, %)

순위	2010년			2011년		
	품목명	금액	전년 대비 증가율	품목명	금액	전년 대비 증가율
	총 계	273,570	17.1	총 계	376,178	37.5
1	자동차부품	32,752	-18.3	원동기 및 펌프	45,785	394.1
2	운반하역기계	26,171	-7.9	육류	43,831	302.7
3	타일 및 도자기제품	19,266	160	타일 및 도자기제품	32,037	66.3
4	정전(static electric)기기	14,933	229.9	자동차부품	23,170	-29.2
5	주단조품	12,438	74.5	운반하역기계	20,103	-23.2
6	육류	10,885	4.1	정전(static electric)기기	13,889	-7
7	기타기계류	9,330	78.1	주단조품	12,269	-1.4
8	원동기 및 펌프	9,266	20.1	유리제품	10,297	1191.9
9	건설광산기계	9,040	98.6	선박해양구조물 및 부품	9,647	9.9
10	선박해양구조물 및 부품	8,779	-23.5	계측제어분석기	9,274	35.6

주: MTI 3단위 기준
자료: 한국무역협회 무역통계

---

3) 한국무역협회(KITA)

□ 2011년 기준 한국의 對폴란드 주요 수출 품목은 평판 디스플레이, 영상기기, 광학기기 및 무선통신기기 등임

□ 영상기기, 광학기기, 반도체 및 자동차 부품 등의 항목은 2010년에 비해 수출이 각각 58.8%, 22.4%, 46.6%, 4.8%의 큰 폭으로 하락함

〈표 I-9〉 최근 對폴란드 10대 수출 품목

(단위: 천달러, %)

순위	2010년			2011년		
	품목명	금액	전년 대비 증가율	품목명	금액	전년 대비 증가율
	총계	4,381,011	5.7	총계	4,100,788	-6.4
1	평판디스플레이 및 센서	1,882,899	-1.4	평판디스플레이 및 센서	1,827,296	-2.9
2	영상기기	545,550	0.9	영상기기	224,610	-58.8
3	무선통신기기	246,384	-2	광학기기	218,929	-10.6
4	광학기기	244,786	82.6	무선통신기기	191,064	-22.4
5	반도체	199,414	86.1	조명기기	153,104	199
6	컴퓨터	151,737	-18	자동차	149,603	112.2
7	자동차부품	139,146	31.5	반도체	106,515	-46.6
8	정전(static electric) 기기	111,754	32	철강판	104,432	17.6
9	철강판	88,781	-14.4	정전(static electric) 기기	103,088	-7.7
10	자동차	70,495	-25.9	자동차부품	90,730	-34.8

주: MTI 3단위 기준
자료: 한국무역협회 무역통계

□ 특히 자동차 부품의 수출 부진은 최근 유럽발 경제위기로 인한 유럽 내 자동차 판매 부진에 기인한다고 볼 수 있음
　○ 폴란드 내 생산된 자동차는 약 98%의 물량이 독일, 이탈리아 및 프랑스 등으로 수출되기 때문에 수입국의 시장 상황에 큰 영향을 받음

○ 2009년 이후 전체 자동차 수출의 30%를 차지하는 이탈리아로의 수출량이 꾸준히 감소하고 있으며 독일로의 수출도 2009년 수출 비중 25%에서 2010년 17%로 급감함

〈표 Ⅰ-10〉 2011년 우리나라의 10대 수출입 국가 순위

(단위: 백만달러)

수 출			수 입		
순위	국가	수출금액	순위	국가	수입금액
1	중국	134,185	1	중국	86,432
2	미국	56,208	2	일본	68,320
3	일본	39,680	3	미국	44,569
4	홍콩	30,968	4	사우디아라비아	36,973
5	싱가포르	20,839	5	카타르	20,749
9	인도	12,654	9	독일	16,963
10	브라질	11,821	10	아랍에미레이트연합	14,759
29	폴란드	4,101	58	폴란드	376

자료: 한국무역협회 무역통계

□ 2011년 기준으로 폴란드는 우리나라의 제29위의 수출상대국, 제58위의 수입 상대국이며 2004년 EU 가입을 전후로 우리나라와의 무역이 최근 6~7년간 비약적으로 증가하였음

4. 폴란드의 자유무역협정(FTA, Free Trade Agreement) 현황

□ 폴란드는 EU 회원국으로서 공동 통상정책에 의거하여 EU가 체결한 특혜 무역협정을 자동적으로 적용받게 됨
   ○ EU 집행위가 27개 회원국으로부터 특정 국가나 지역과의 지역무역협정 협상권을 위임받아 제3국가와 체결한 협정은 EU 27개국 모두에 자동 적용됨

□ EU는 전통적으로 FTA협상에서 정치적·외교적인 동기에 의거하여 지역 대 지역 협

상을 선호해 왔으나 1991년을 기점으로 상업적인 목적하에 개별국과의 양자간 협정을 본격적으로 시작함
  ○ 최근 WTO DDA협상이 난항을 겪으며 FTA 추진에 더욱 적극적인 자세를 보여주고 있음

□ WTO로부터 지역무역협정으로 인정받기 위해 EU는 FTA협정을 맺을 경우 양측 상품 무역의 90% 이상의 관세 철폐를 선호함

□ EU는 지난 2006년 10월 '신통상정책'을 선언하면서 FTA 우선추진 대상국으로 한국, 인도, ASEAN,[4] 러시아, MERCOSUR(남미공동시장),[5] GCC(걸프협력회의)[6]를 선정한 바 있음
  ○ ASEAN의 경우 당초 목표로 했던 ASEAN 전체와의 협상을 중단하고 싱가포르, 말레이시아와의 양자간 협상을 개시하였으며 베트남과의 협상 개시를 검토 중임
  ○ 인도는 2007년 6월에 협상이 개시되어 2012년 6월까지 11차 고위 협상이 진행되었음
  ○ 캐나다는 2009월 5월에 협상이 개시되어 2009년 6월에 상호경제무역협정(CETA, Comprehensive Economic and Trade Agreement)에 합의하였으며 2012년 현재까지 9차 협상을 진행하였음
  ○ 2010년 2월 콜롬비아 및 페루와 무역협정 체결을 위한 협상을 개시하였으며 EU 집행위에서 채택된 협정안이 2012년 2월 EU 대외무역장관이사회에서 서명되어 EU 의회의 승인 절차만 남겨놓고 있음

---

[4] 동남아시아 지역 협력을 위한 국가 연합으로 태국, 인도네시아, 필리핀, 말레이시아, 싱가포르, 베트남, 라오스, 미얀마, 캄보디아, 브루나이가 가입되어 있음
[5] 브라질, 아르헨티나, 우루과이, 파라과이 등 남미 4개국 공동시장임
[6] 페르시아만 연안국의 안보, 경제협력을 위한 국가연합으로서 사우디아라비아, 쿠웨이트, 아랍에미리트, 카타르, 오만, 바레인 등 6개국이 가입되어 있음

〈표 Ⅰ-11〉 한국 및 EU(폴란드)의 자유 무역 협정 현황

	한국	한국과 EU공통	EU
발효	싱가포르 (2006년 3월) ASEAN (2009년 9월) 인도 (2010년 1월) 페루 (2011년 8월) 미국 (2012년 3월)	칠레 (한국: 2004년 4월 EU: 2003년 2월) EFTA (한국: 2006년 9월 EU: 1994년 1월) 한·EU FTA (2011년 7월)	OCTs(1971년 1월), 스위스·리히텐슈타인(1973년1월), 아이슬란드(1973년 4월), 노르웨이(1973년 7월), 시리아(1977년 7월), EEA(1994년 1월), 터키(1996년 1월), Faroe Islands[7](1997년 1월), Plastinian Authority(1997년 7월), 튀니지(1998년 3월), 남아프리카공화국(2000년 1월), 모로코(2000년 3월), 이스라엘(2000년 6월), 멕시코(2000년 7월), 마케도니아(2001년 6월), 크로아티아(2002년 3월), 요르단(2002년 5월), 레바논(2003년 3월), 이집트(2004년 6월), 알제리(2005년 9월), 알바니아(2006년 12월), 몬테네그로(2008년 1월), 보스니아, 헤르체고비나(2008년 7월), CARIFORUM States[1](2008년 11월), 코트디부아르(2009년 1월), 카메룬(2009년 10월), 세르비아(2010년 2월)
협상 진행	터키, 멕시코, 인도네시아, 중국, 콜롬비아, 뉴질랜드, 호주, 호주 등	GCC, 캐나다 등	인도, MERCOSUR, 우크라이나, 콜롬비아, 리비아, 에콰도르 등
검토	MERCOSUR, 이스라엘, 몽골, 말레이시아 등	중국, 일본, 러시아 등	파키스탄, 싱가포르, 이라크, 베트남, 인도네시아, 아르메니아, 아제르바이잔, 코소보, 벨라루스, 카자흐스탄, 파키스탄, 몰도바, 그루지아 등

주: 1) 카리브해 연안 중남미 국가들의 연합
자료: WTO(www.wto.org), KITA(한국무역협회),
　　　외교통상부 한·EU FTA 포털(http://www.fta.go.kr/eu)

○ MERCOSUR와의 협상 지침은 1999년에 채택되었으나 여러 차례 협상이 중단되었다가 2010년 5월에 양측 간 협상이 공식 재개되었음
　- 2010년 5월 이후 2012년 3월까지 8차례 협상이 진행되었음

---

7) 스코틀랜드와 아이슬란드, 그리고 노르웨이의 중간에 위치한 18개의 섬

□ 2009년 한·EU 협상 종료 후, 2010년 9월 16일 협정안이 승인되어 2011년 7월 1일 한·EU FTA가 발효됨
  ○ 한·EU 협정문 및 관련 설명 자료는 한·EU FTA 포털 사이트[8])에서 열람이 가능함

□ 폴란드는 연간 80만대의 중고차를 수입하는 시장이기 때문에 한·EU FTA가 발효됨으로써 관세 혜택으로 인한 한국 자동차 수출이 촉진될 것으로 예상됨
  ○ 한·EU 원산지 규정은 자동차 및 자동차 부품 생산에서 역외산 허용치를 45%와 50%로 하기 때문에 중국이나 인도로부터 저렴한 부품 조달이 용이한 한국산 자동차가 가격 경쟁력을 가질 것으로 예상됨
  ○ 그러나 유럽 재정위기로 인한 자동차 수요 감소에 따라 저렴하면서 고품질을 찾는 수요가 늘어날 것이므로 한국 차 선호도 제고를 위한 홍보 전략 마련이 필요함

□ LDPE, PVC 등 일부 제품을 제외하고는 EU 자체 공급이 부족하기 때문에 폴란드의 대량 수입제품(폴리에틸렌, 폴리프로필렌, EPS 등)을 중심으로 우리 제품의 수출이 유망할 것임

5. 폴란드의 AEO 제도[9])

□ AEO(Authorized Economic Operator) 프로그램은 유럽 공동체(EC) 역내 무역 원활화 및 국제수출통제 기준 이행을 조화롭게 해결하기 위해 도입됨

□ 세계관세기구(WCO, World Customs Organization)의 Safe Framework에 의해 권장되고 있는 제도이며 미국 세관보안제도인 C-TPAT에 상응함
  ○ AEO는 강제적인 제도가 아닌 민간업체의 자발적인 협력으로 운영함

---

8) http://www.fta.go.kr/eu/main/index.asp
9) 산업자원부 보도자료 2005.11.8

□ EU 의회는 EC통관규정 648/2005[10])에 따라 AEO제도를 운영하고 있음
  ○ 이 개정은 역내 안전과 안보를 확보할 수 있도록 통관 규정을 개정했다는 의미로 안보개정(Security Amendment)이라고 부르고 있음
  ○ 수출통제물자의 국제적 통제기준 이행 및 위험요소 제거를 위해 기업과 세관이 협력하여 통관절차 간소화에 기할 수 있는 발판을 마련했다는 의미가 있음

□ 인증 심사 기준은 EU 회원국 모두 동일하나, 국가별로 심사주체가 다르며 역내 한 회원국에서 인증받은 기업은 다른 회원국에서도 차별 없이 혜택을 부여받음
  ○ 폴란드의 경우 모든 세관이 심사 주체로서 심사 권한을 부여받았음

□ 공인 대상 업체는 제조, 수출, 포워딩, 창고, 관세사, 운송, 수입자로 구분하며 AEO C (통관절차 신속), AEO S(보안), AEO F(통관절차 신속 및 보안) 방식으로 운영 중임

□ 통관과 관련해 정해진 기준에 따라 신뢰를 인정받은 기업은 관세청에서 AEO 인증마크를 받을 수 있음
  ○ 통상 3년간의 통관요건을 준수했다는 기록과 건전한 재무상태, 적절한 내부통제가 가능한 조직, 적절한 안전 및 안보 여건에 대한 확인이 인증 부여 요건임
  ○ EU 내에 사무소를 가지고 있으며 통관 간소화 절차를 완료한 항공 및 선박 운송업자인 경우 참여 가능함

□ AEO인증을 받은 기업은 통관 간소화, 통관 절차 면제, 안보통제 신속화의 혜택을 받게 됨
  ○ 역내 세관 간 약식신고서(summary declaration) 교환으로, 물자의 국경통과 때마다 중복적 신고를 대체할 수 있음
  ○ 저위험 업체로 등록되어 서류 및 육안 검사가 경감되며 화물 검색 시 우선 처리됨
  ○ 통관검색 위치를 자율적으로 지정할 수 있어 원하는 곳에서 적은 비용 혹은 빠른 절차로 통관 검색이 가능함

---

10) http://eur-lex.europa.eu/LexUriServ/LexUriServ.do?uri=OJ:L:2005:117:0013:0019:en:PDF 에서 참조

○ 통관 간소화 절차가 무심사로 통과되고 통관절차 결과 통보 순위의 선순위로 배정됨
○ 관세청과 협력관계가 향상되며 필요 시 추가적으로 구체적 정보 및 기록의 공유가 허용됨

□ 인증에 대한 별도의 유효기간은 없으나 EU 관련 법령의 주요사항 개정 시 또는 인증 기업이 AEO기준에 더 이상 부합하지 못한다는 합리적 징후가 있을 경우 담당부처가 재심사할 수 있음

□ EU의 AEO는 수입부문에만 신청할 수 있는 미국 세관보안제도인 C-TPAT와는 다르게 수출부문에 대해서도 신청할 수 있는 특징을 가지고 있음

□ 정식시행은 2009년 1월에 EU 내 전 국가로 확대하였으며 2012년 3월 기준 EU 27개국 9,068개 기업이 인증을 획득함

□ EU의 AEO승인을 획득한 업체에 대한 정보와 승인 세관에 대한 정보는 EU 위원회 홈페이지[11]에서 확인할 수 있음

□ 각국은 국가 간의 AEO제도를 상호 인정하는 제도로서 MRA(Mutual Recognition Arrangement)를 체결하고 있으며 중복적인 시험의 방지, 불필요한 규제 비용 절감, 교역을 위한 시장 접근의 용이성 향상 등의 효과가 있음

□ 우리나라는 일본, 미국, 싱가포르, 뉴질랜드 등과 MRA를 체결하고 있으며 2012년 현재 EU와의 MRA체결을 가속화하고 있음

---

11) http://ec.europa.eu/taxation_customs/dds2/eos/aeo_home.jsp?Lang=en

<표 I-12> 우리나라의 MRA체결 현황

구분	국가	체결일	발효일
체결완료	미국	2010. 06. 25	2010. 09. 01
	싱가포르	2010. 06. 25	2011. 01. 01
	캐나다	2010. 06. 25	미 발효
	일본	2011. 05. 20	2011. 11. 01
	뉴질랜드	2011. 06. 25	2012. 01. 01
추진 중	중국, EU	(EU는 2012년 내로 추진 예정)	

자료: WCO, AEO Compendium, 2011 및 관세청 발표자료

□ 한국과 EU는 1997년 세관상호지원협정을 체결하여 관세범의 조사공조, 기술협력, 정보의 요청, 비용부담 등에 대한 협의로 원활환 통관을 위해 노력하고 있음
  ○ EU는 한국과 세관상호협정을 체결한 후 2년 주기로 세관협력회의를 개최하였으며 제6, 7차 세관협력회의에서 MRA 체결에 대한 논의가 본격적으로 이루어졌음

II. 외국의 통상환경 보고서

1. World Bank의 「Doing Business 2013」

□ 세계은행(The World Bank)은 2004년부터 매년 '사업하기 좋은 나라(Ease of doing business)' 순위를 다양한 부문에 걸쳐 조사하여 「Doing Business」라는 보고서명으로 발표하고 있음
  ○ 2013년에 발간된 「Doing Business 2013」는 2012년 한 해 동안 185개국에 대하여 부문별로 조사·평가한 내용이 수록됨
  ○ 「Doing Business 2013」 보고서상 순위를 결정짓기 위하여 조사된 분야는 사업 개시(Starting a business), 건설 허가(Dealing with construction permits), 전력 수신(Getting electricity), 부동산 취득(Registering property), 신용 취득(Getting credit), 투자자 보호(Protecting investors), 세금 납부(Paying taxes), 무역(Trading across borders), 계약 이행(Enforcing contract) 및 청산(Resolving insolvency) 등 10개의 지표임
  ○ 2013년 보고서에 따르면, 종합적인 '사업의 용이성(Ease of Doing Business)' 순위에 있어 싱가포르가 1위를 차지하였으며, 우리나라는 8위에 올랐음

□ 당해 보고서의 무역 분야 순위는 수출입에 필요한 서류의 개수와 수출입 소요 일수 및 소요 비용 등을 산출하여 순위를 정하고 있으며, 필요서류가 적고 수출입 소요 기일이 짧을수록 더욱 높은 순위에 오르는 형식임
  ○ 무역 분야에서 2012년 보고서상 4위에 올랐던 우리나라는 2013년 보고서에서는 1계단 상승하여 3위에 오름

<표 Ⅱ-1> 「Doing Business 2013」 폴란드의 무역 분야 순위 비교

구분	폴란드	동유럽 및 중앙아시아 (평균)	OECD (평균)	러시아	체코	한국
수출필요서류(개수)	5	7	4	8	4	3
수출소요시간(일)	17	26	10	21	16	7
수출소요비용 (달러/컨테이너)	1,050	2,134	1,028	2,820	1,145	665
수입필요서류(개수)	5	8	5	11	7	3
수입소요시간(일)	16	29	10	36	17	7
수입소요비용 (달러/컨테이너)	1,025	2,349	1,080	2,920	1,180	695
무역 분야 순위	50	-	-	162	68	3

자료: The World Bank, 「Doing Business 2013」

□ 「Doing Business 2013」 폴란드의 종합 순위는 185국 중 55위로, 지난해보다 19순위 상승하였으며 무역 부문(Trading Across Borders)은 50위로 지난해 49위에서 1순위 하락하였음
  ○ 폴란드는 무역 부문을 제외한 사업 개시, 부동산 취득, 세금 납부, 계약 이행 및 청산 등 대부분의 분야에서 순위가 상승하였음

<표 Ⅱ-2> 폴란드 수출입 소요 기간 및 비용

(단위: 일, 달러)

구 분	수출		수입	
	소요기간	비용	소요기간	비용
서류준비	10	145	10	120
세관통관	1	65	2	65
항만(터미널)	3	140	2	140
내륙운송	3	700	2	700
합 계	17	1,050	16	1,025

자료: The World Bank, 「Doing Business 2013, Poland」

□ 폴란드에서 해상 수출을 위해 소요되는 비용은 컨테이너당12) 약 1,050달러이며, 수출에 필요한 서류는 5가지이고, 서류 준비, 수출통관, 국내 운송, 항만업무 등 수출이 이루어지는 단계에서 총 17일이 소요되는 것으로 조사됨

□ 해상 수입에 있어서 컨테이너당 약 1,025달러의 금액이 소요되며, 수입에 필요한 서류는 5가지이고, 서류 준비, 수입통관, 국내 운송, 항만 업무 등 수입이 이루어지는 단계에서 총 16일 소요됨

□ 폴란드의 수출입에 필요한 기본적인 서류는 선하증권, 상업 송장, 원산지 증명, 수출입 신고서, 포장명세서임

□ 「Doing Business 2013」에 따르면 폴란드는 통관서류의 준비 및 제출 과정의 전자화를 실시하여 통관 속도가 비교적 빨라짐

2. 미국 국별 무역장벽 보고서(National Trade Estimate Report on Foreign Trade Barriers: NTE 보고서)

□ 국별 무역장벽보고서는 1974년 통상법(Trade Act of 1974) 제181조에 근거하여 미국 무역대표부(USTR, United States Trade Representative)가 작성, 매년 3월 말 의회에 제출하는 연례 보고서임
  ○ 이 보고서는 미국 업계의 의견과 해외 주재 미국 대사관의 보고서와 관련 정부부처의 의견 등을 기초로 작성됨
  ○ 2012년 보고서는 미국의 62개 주요 교역국 및 경제권의 무역과 투자 장벽에 대해 포괄적으로 기술하고 있음13)

---

12) 20피트 컨테이너(TEU) 만재화물 기준이며, 위험물 또는 군수품 등이 아니라는 가정하에 금액을 산정함
13) 2010년부터 동식물 위생 및 검역(SPS, Sanitary and Phytosanitary Measures) 및 무역에 대한 기술 장벽(TBT, Technical Barriers to Trade) 관련 사안은 NTE 보고서와 별도로 발표하고 있음

□ 폴란드는 2004년까지는 국별 보고서로 개별 출간되었으나 2005년부터는 EU보고서 내에 통합됨
  ○ 국별 보고서는 분야별 관세 장벽과 비관세 장벽으로 나누어 수입 허가, 수량 제한, 제품 등록 등에 대해 서술하는 것이 일반적임
  ○ 2012년 EU의 경우 비농산물, 농산물 시장 접근성 및 지적재산권 보호, 서비스 장벽, 투자 장벽, 정부 조달, 보조금 지원, 관세행정기관과 전자상거래로 나누어 EU 전체 및 국가별 특징을 기술함

□ 무역 개관 부분에서는 EU 전체의 무역현황에 대해 설명하고 있으며 EU가 미국의 두 번째 수출 시장이라는 것과, 양국 간의 수출입 규모 증가 추세를 언급함
  ○ 2011년 미국의 對EU 무역 적자는 전년 대비 12억 천만달러 증가한 99억 2천만달러를 기록하였음
    - 對EU 미국 수출은 239억 8천만달러로 전년 대비 15.2% 상승하였음
  ○ 미국의 對EU 개인 상업 서비스(Private Commercial Service) 수출은 2009년 169억 천만달러이었고, 수입은 125억 4천만달러였음
    - EU 내 미국 주요 계열회사의 서비스 판매액은 2008년 508억 5천만달러였던 반면, 미국 내 EU 주요 계열사의 서비스 판매액은 373억 1천만달러였음
  ○ EU에 대한 미국의 해외직접투자(FDI, foreign direct investment) 주식 자본은 2010년 1조 9천억달러로 2009년 1조 8천억달러 대비 1천억달러가 증가하였음
  ○ 미국의 FDI는 주로 비은행계 지주 회사와 금융 및 보험 그리고 제조업 분야에 집중됨

가. 비농산물 시장 접근성

1) WTO 정보기술협정(Information Technology Agreement)

□ WTO ITA 위반에 대한 미국과 EU의 분쟁에서 WTO분쟁해결기구(Dispute Settlement Body)가 미국의 손을 들어줌으로써 첨단 기술 제품의 EU 내 무관세 수출이 가능하게 됨

- EU는 평면 컴퓨터 판넬 모니터와 다기능 프린터를 비롯하여 특정 케이블과 위성, 디지털 위성방송 수신기 등에 대해 14%의 관세를 부과하였으나 미국이 이에 이의를 제기함
- 2010년 9월 WTO가 마지막 패널 보고서를 승인하였고 EU에 부과한 9개월 9일간의 유예기간이 지난 2011년 6월 3일 만료됨으로써 미국 최첨단 제품들을 무관세로 EU에 수출할 수 있게 되었음

2) 의약품

□ 미국은 폴란드 정부에 의약품 상환제도와 약가 설정방법에 대한 정책 개발 및 투명성 확보를 요구함
  - 폴란드뿐 아니라 독일, 헝가리, 리투아니아, 네덜란드, 포르투갈, 스페인 영국과 같은 EU 국가들의 의약품 시장 접근성 및 제도적 투명성 확보를 권고함

나. 농산물 시장 접근성

1) 바나나

□ EU는 2009년 12월 개시된 협정을 통해 바나나 무역 시 관세 부과 이외의 다른 차별화된 조치를 취하지 않을 것임을 약속함
  - EU는 바나나 수입 시 국가에 따라 차별화된 무역 레짐을 적용하고 있었음
  - EU는 바나나를 공급하는 남미 국가들과 이미 바나나 무역에 관한 제네바 협정(GATB, Geneva Agreement on Trade in Bananas)을 맺고 있었으나 미국과 남미 국가들 모두 2010년 6월 EU와의 새로운 협정에 동의함
  - EU는 이 협정에 대한 국내 비준이 완료되면 바나나에 부과하는 새로운 관세에 대한 WTO의 공식적 인증을 요청할 것임

2) 현미

☐ 미국은 2005년 발효된 현미 협정에서 기준 체적을 증가시키고 양허관세보다 낮은 비율의 관세를 부과하여 지속적으로 시장 접근성을 유지하려고함
  ○ 일반적으로 WTO 규칙하에서는 톤당 65유로 이상의 관세를 부과할 수 없음

3) Meursing Table Tariff Code

☐ 제과 관련 제품, 조리된(구운) 제품 그리고 기타 보조식품은 EU의 특정 분류체계에 따르며 특히 각 제품의 특정 성분에 따라 각각 다른 비율의 관세를 부과함
  ○ 제품의 유단백질, 유지방, 전분 그리고 설탕 함유량에 따라 제품 각각에 차별화된 관세를 부과함
  ○ 따라서 수출국은 제품의 성분을 측정하여 부과될 관세를 계산해야 하기 때문에 행정적 불편을 겪음

4) 생명공학 농산품

☐ 2009년 NTE보고서에 따르면 폴란드 정부는 사료에 포함되는 생명공학 작물들에 대한 수입 금지 조치를 2012년까지 연장하였음

다. 지적재산권의 보호

☐ 폴란드는 2008년부터 2010년까지 지적재산권 보호 강화를 위한 국가 액션 플랜을 이행하여 미국무역대표부(USTR)가 발행한 2010 스페셜 301조 보고서(Special 301 Report)의 감시 대상국(Watch List)에서 제외됨(2011년 보고서)

☐ 폴란드 정부는 EU의 지식재산권 보호 전략을 포함된 2011년부터 2013년까지의 새로운 국가 액션 플랜을 발표하였으며 지적재산권 법 집행 강화를 위한 표준 플랫폼

을 구축 중에 있음

라. 서비스 장벽 (금융서비스)

□ 폴란드는 외국 금융서비스 제공자들로부터 연결부가가치세제도(VAT Grouping)[14]의 도입을 지속적으로 요구받아 왔으나 2010년까지 도입하지 않았음
  ○ 영국, 네덜란드, 아일랜드, 독일, 오스트리아, 덴마크, 핀란드, 스웨덴, 루마니아, 스페인, 벨기에, 헝가리 그리고 체코는 이미 연결부가가치세제도를 시행하고 있음(2010년 보고서)

마. 세관 행정

□ EU 전체 국가의 세관 행정을 관리하는 단일 기관이 없으며 따라서 각 나라마다 EU의 관세법을 다른 방식으로 받아들여 집행하고 있음
  ○ EU법 적용에 대해 유럽재판소(ECJ, European Court of Justice)의 결정은 구속력이 없기 때문에 관세와 관련된 행정 문제를 바로잡는 것은 다소 길고 복잡한 과정을 필요로 함

□ 2008년 EU 집행위원회는 관세분야에 대한 미래 발전전략의 기본 틀을 제안하였음
  ○ 특히 관세코드의 현대화(MCCC, Modernized Community Customs Code)를 통해 통관절차의 간소화를 추구하고 있으며 이는 2013년 완료될 예정임
  ○ 몇몇의 현대화된 관세 코드가 EORI 번호(EORI number)에 사용되고 있으며 이는 또한 기존의 Regulation 2913/92를 대체할 것임

---

14) 법적으로 독립된 납세자들이 재무적·경제적·조직적으로 밀접하게 연관되어 있다면 그 경제적 단일체를 하나의 부가가치세 납세의무자로 간주하는 것

Ⅲ. 폴란드의 통관 환경

1. 통관행정 개요

가. 통관행정 조직

1) EU 통관행정 조직

☐ 폴란드는 2004년 7월부터 EU 회원국으로써 EU 집행위의 절차 및 관세 법령을 따르고 있음

☐ EU는 EU 집행위(Commission) 관세총국(Taxation and Customs Union)과 27개 회원국 세관당국의 2중 구조로 이루어져 있음15)
- ○ EU 집행위 관세총국에서 EU 회원국의 수출입 통관행정을 총괄하고 있으며 Director-General 산하 5명의 Director로 구성되어 있음
- ○ Directorate A는 통관정책 및 전자세관, 통관규정 및 세관 간 일치, 통관절차, 품목분류, 관세율 및 감면에 대한 업무를 담당함
- ○ Directorate B는 IPR(지식재산권) 및 위험관리 및 보안, 원산지, 국제협력에 대한 업무를 담당하고 있음

☐ EU 집행위는 중앙정부로서 통관 관련 규정 등의 제·개정, 세관당국 간 이견 조정, 통관행정 발전방향 수립 등의 역할을 수행하고 있음
- ○ 그러나 개별 회원국 세관당국에 따라 원산지, 품목분류 등의 판단이나 통관의 신속성, 정확성 등에서 차이가 발생함

---

15) 2012년 해외통관제도 설명회, 관세청

- 따라서 EU 전체의 관세법령뿐 아니라, 개별 회원국 세부적 업무처리 절차 및 관행 등에 대해서는 각 국가의 지침을 따라야함

2) 폴란드 통관행정 조직

[그림 Ⅲ-1] 폴란드 관세행정 조직도

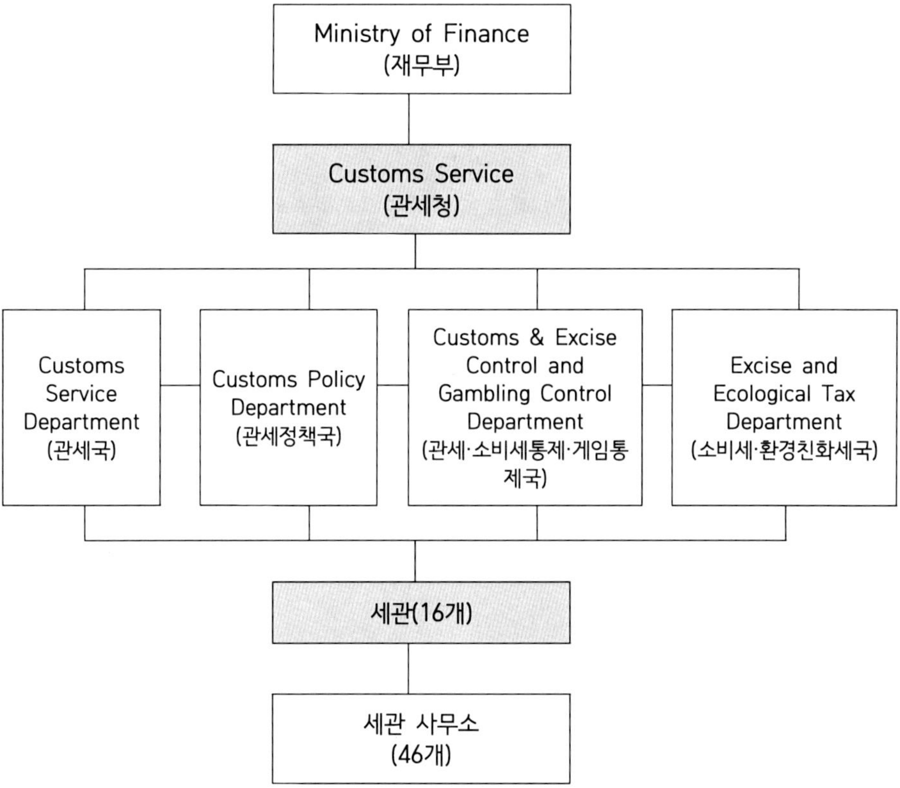

```
              Ministry of Finance
                   (재무부)
                      │
              Customs Service
                   (관세청)
     ┌──────────┬──────────┼──────────┬──────────┐
  Customs    Customs Policy  Customs & Excise   Excise and
  Service    Department      Control and        Ecological Tax
  Department (관세정책국)    Gambling Control   Department
  (관세국)                   Department         (소비세·환경친화세국)
                             (관세·소비세통제·게임통
                              제국)
                      │
                  세관(16개)
                      │
                  세관 사무소
                    (46개)
```

자료: 관세청

□ 기존의 관세 책임을 지고 있던 관세 중앙위원회가 2002년 5월 1일자로 활동을 중지하여 중앙 정부 사무소를 구성하는 관세 책임은 재무부로 이관되었음

□ 폴란드 관세청(Customs Service)은 재무부 산하 독립외청으로 국제 상업교류 대상

관세 통제, 국경에서 부과된 관세 및 조세평가 및 징수(수입 VAT, 소비세) 밀수입 대응 및 관세 사기 방지 등의 임무를 수행함
  ○ 관세청이 담당하는 업무는 크게 국가산업 보호 및 자연환경, 소비자, 사회, 문화 등을 보호하는 업무와 지역 내 통제업무 및 관세청 협력 기관을 관리하는 업무의 세 가지로 분류할 수 있음

□ 폴란드 관세청은 관세국(Department of Customs Service), 관세정책국(Customs Policy Department), 관세·소비세통제·게임통제국(Customs & Excise Control and Gambling Control Department), 소비세·환경친화세국(Excise and Ecological Tax Department)의 4개 관련부처로 구성됨
  ○ 관세정책국이 관세법을 입안하고, 관세청은 관세국의 법률 자문 서비스를 받아 직무를 수행함
  ○ 관세국에서는 조직, 예산, 인사, 통계 및 관세 서비스 촉진 관련 이슈를 관할하며 도박과 관련한 정부의 정책 수단을 준비하고 전자세관의 이행을 감시함
  ○ 관세·소비세·게임 통제국에서는 관세법, 소비세, 도박세, 석유비의 범위를 통제하며 감사 및 감찰, 범죄 및 범법행위 처리, 국세범죄 처리를 감독하고 통제함
  ○ 소비세·환경친화세국에서는 소비세, 환경세, 기타 유사 조세정책을 수행하며 소비세 상품과 승용차 시장을 감시하고 소비세와 관련한 IT시스템 운영과 적용을 독립적으로 감독함

□ 16개 세관(Customs Chambers)이 무역과 관련한 업무 전반을 지원하고 있으며 각 세관의 세관장이 통관 애로사항 해소를 위한 실질적인 권한을 가지고 있음
  ○ 세관 하위에 세관 사무소(46개) 및 출장소(160개)가 해당 지역 및 국경지대의 세관 업무를 담당하고 있음

□ 관세청은 통관 과정의 효율성 확보, 지역 세관과의 원활한 소통, 위기관리 능력, 세관의 전산화 및 현대화 등에 대한 개선방안인 Action Strategy of Polish Customs 2010-2015를 발표함[16]

□ 폴란드의 재무부가 수입 허가와 금지 그리고 쿼터와 규제를 관할하지만 다른 정부부처 또한 특별한 사법적 관할권을 가지고 있음
  ○ 담배는 농산부가, 상공·해양 그리고 토지 교통에 관한 부분은 교통부, 천연자원의 수출입은 환경보호부가 관할하고 해당 제품에 수입허가서를 발부함

□ 폴란드 관세청은 공식 관세브라우저(ISZTAR)가 있으며 관세브라우저는 세관행정 및 무역업체들에 국제무역 제품에 관한 정보를 제공함
  ○ 관세브라우저는 TARIC(EU 관세분류번호)이 제공하는 정보(제품의 명칭, 관세율, 제약, 관세쿼터, 관세 상한 및 보류)뿐 아니라 국내 정보(VAT, 소비세, 제약, 비관세 조치) 또한 제시함
  ○ 뿐만 아니라 관세행정기관과 모든 관련기관에 상품의 총매출액과 관련된 세부적인 정보를 제공함
  ○ TARIC 데이터베이스에 통합되지 않은 일부 국가의 비관세 조치도 관세브라우저를 통해 파악할 수 있음

□ 폴란드 세관은 수입 신고를 간편화하기 위한 전산화된 세관 신고 시스템인 CELINA를 운영하고 있음
  ○ CELINA를 통한 수입 신고 정보는 EU 내 IT시스템과는 개별적으로 처리되며 전자 신고에 대한 안내와 규정은 폴란드 세관 홈페이지[17])에서 가능함
  ○ 이 시스템을 통한 수출 신고는 불가능함

---

16) http://www.mofnet.gov.pl/_files_/sluzba_celna/strategia/customs_action_strategy_sc_2015_+_2_.pdf에서 다운받을 수 있음

17) http://www.mofnet.gov.pl/index.php?const=2&dzial=420&wysw=2&sub=sub7

나. 각종 수입 허가제도

1) 품목분류 사전 심사제도(BTI) 및 품목분류에 관한 규정[18]

☐ 품목분류 사전 심사제도(BTI, Binding Tariff Information)는 수출입업체의 신청에 의하여 관세청장이 수출입물품에 적용될 품목분류를 결정하여 통보해주는 제도임
  ○ 업체 스스로 품목분류 및 관세율을 정하여 세금을 납부하는 '신고납부제'하에서 업체 스스로 품목분류를 결정하기가 어려운 경우 공식적 품목분류 통보를 통해 업무의 효율성을 높일 수 있음
  ○ 통보되는 품목분류는 일정한 사유로 인하여 변경되는 경우에도 변경 시점까지는 기통보된 품목분류가 적용되므로 관세 추징 및 이에 따른 불복청구 절차 등 업체의 부담을 근본적으로 예방할 수 있음
  ○ 특히 최근 IT 상품은 첨단화, 복합, 다기능화되고 있어 품목분류상 쟁점이 계속 발생할 수 있는 분야이기 때문에 BTI를 통해 관세 분쟁을 예방하는 것이 바람직함

☐ EU는 Council Regulation (EEC) 2913/92 of 12와 Commission Regulation (EEC) No. 2454/93 of 2에 의거하여 BTI를 실시하고 있으며 신청자는 상기 관세법령에 규정된 서면양식으로 교부를 신청해야 함[19]

☐ 복합품목분류표 외에 주해서를 운용하여 품목분류에 참고토록 하고 있으며, 가장 최신 해설서는 2011년 5월 6일자 관보에 개재된 Explanatory notes to the Combined Nomenclature of the European Union[20]임

☐ Council Regulation (EEC) Non 2658/87에 의하면 EU 회원국의 요청 또는 관세총국

---

[18] 2012년 관세관 해외통관제도 설명회
[19] http://ec.europa.eu/taxation_customs/customs/customs_duties/tariff_aspects/classification_goods/index_en.htm#bti_application_form에서 관련 법령 및 신청서를 다운받을 수 있음
[20] http://eur-lex.europa.eu/LexUriServ/LexUriServ.do?uri=OJ:C:2011:137:0001:0397:EN:PDF에서 확인 가능

의 판단 등에 의해 총국 내에 설치되어 있는 관세규정위원회(Customs Code Committee)에 27개 회원국 대표가 참여하여 복합품목분류표의 제·개정을 수행함

☐ 세관 당국은 가장 빠른 기간 내에(as soon as possible) 품목분류 결과를 서면으로 통지해야하며 접수일 이후 3개월 내 정보 제공을 못할 경우, 지연사유 및 통지 기간을 알려주어야 함

☐ BTI는 동일한 조건하에 모든 회원국을 구속하며, 효력 범위는 동 정보의 소지자에 대해서만, 또한 정보가 제공된 날 이후에 세관 절차를 완료하는 물품에 대해서만 세관당국을 구속할 수 있음
  ○ BTI는 교부된 날로부터 6년간 유효하나, 만일 신청자에 의해 부정확 혹은 불충분한 정보가 제공된 때에는 무효가 됨

☐ 27개 회원국의 관세수입 75%가 EU 집행위 예산으로 산입되어 품목분류 시 상황 변화 고려보다는 관세수입 확보 목적으로 보수적인 접근 방식을 취하므로 업체에는 유리하지 않은 입장임

  2) 라벨링(Labelling)

☐ 라벨에는 모든 필수 정보들 (제품의 이름, 명칭, 포장자 혹은 수입자, 배포자, 원산지, 제품 구성요소, 견고함, 순중량 등)이 폴란드어로 기입되어 있어야 함
  ○ 수입자의 성명이나 주소, 로트 번호와 같은 정보는 라벨에 표기하지 않음
  ○ 다국적 언어로 된 라벨도 수용이 되나 폴란드어가 함께 표기되어 있어야 함

☐ 포장 및 라벨링은 특정한 제품을 제외하고 EU의 라벨링 규정을 따라야 하며 또한 원산지 기준을 충족해야 함

☐ 소비재의 경우 제품 설명서가 포장 내부 혹은 외부에 표시되어 있어야 함

□ 식품첨가물에 대한 정보는 성분표에 표기되어야 하고 음식 알레르기 및 영양소에 관한 정보 또한 표기되어야 함

□ 포장제품 혹은 통조림제품에는 제품성분, 영양성분, 유통기일, 제조자의 성명 및 주소, 제품 무게 등을 폴란드어로 표기해야 하며 포장작업이 이루어진 국가가 명백하게 표시되어 있어야 함

□ 폴란드는 헤어 케어 제품에 대한 특정한 라벨링을 가지고 있으며 제품의 무역명과 종류, 수입자 혹은 제조자의 이름과 주소, 포장 단위별 용량, 유효기간, 로트번호, 성분 목록, 원산지 등이 표시되어 있어야 함[21]

□ 이미 다른 EU 국가에서 승인을 받았다면, 제품이 승인된 국가의 제품 확인 증명서를 세관에 제시함으로써 통관이 가능함

3) 기타 특수 인증

□ 농산물 가격보조 제도인 공동농업정책(CAP, Common Agriculture Policy) 수입면허는 미국과 같은 제3국에서 EU국가로 해당 농산물을 수입할 시 허가함
  ○ 흔히 C증명서라고 불리는 수입면허는 폴란드 농산물 유통공사(Agricultural Market Agency)가 발행함

□ 화장품과 관련하여 신규 화장품을 폴란드로 수입하거나 제조하여 폴란드에서 판매할 때에는 수입자가 반드시 폴란드 화장품 등록기관(The National Registration System for Cosmetic Products)에 등록해야 함
  ○ 과거에는 신규 화장품의 제조와 판매에 대해 PZH(폴란드 위생청)에서 인증을 받아야 했으나 EU 가입에 따라 현재 의무 인증은 없음
  ○ PZH 인증은 폴란드인에게 친숙하여 신뢰성을 줄 수 있으나 많은 비용과 시간

---

21) EDC, Dubai Export Development Corporation, Exporting to Poland 2009.10

이 소모되는 단점이 있음

□ 공산품과 관련하여 폴란드는 EU 회원국 전체에 적용되는 강제 기술규격 인증인 CE(Communaute Europeen)를 따라야 함
  ○ CE는 공산품에 대해 EU 회원국 전체에 적용되며 27개 EU 회원국과 스위스, 노르웨이, 아이슬란드의 EFTA국가에 수출하려면 CE를 부착해야만 함
  ○ CE를 따르면서 폴란드가 기존에 사용하던 강제인증 제도인 PCBC(Polish Center for Testing and Certification)의 B마크(B safety)는 그 기능을 상실함[22]
  ○ 소비자 건강, 안전, 위생 및 환경보호와 관련한 제품의 폴란드 내 수입 및 판매를 위해서는 CE마킹 지침(83/68EEC)에 의거하여 22개 카테고리의 품목에 CE마크를 부착해야 함
  ○ 자세한 내용은 http://certinfo.korcham.net/Client/Product/ProductCert.aspx?idx=1 → 해외제품 인증 → 유럽 선택 → CE 및 기타 인증 절차 및 사후관리에서 확인 가능함

□ CE마크 획득에 걸리는 시간은 제품의 기술적 복잡성과 검사 항목에 따라 다르며 획득 비용 및 소요기간의 경우도 제품의 복잡성과 제품군별에 따라 다름
  ○ 단, 이미 판매 허가된 장비에 한해 기존 허가 일시를 인정하며 가입일 이후 수입 및 판매되는 새 장비의 경우 일정한 '경과기간'을 인정해 줌

□ 폴란드 인증센터(Polish Centre for Accreditation) 및 폴란드 표준위원회(Polish Committee for Standardization)가 CE마크에 대한 승인을 주로 담당함
  ○ 이 밖에도 폴란드 경제, 노동, 사회 정책부(Ministry of Economy, Labor & Social Policy), 소비자 보호 사무소(Office for Competition and Consumer Protection) 및 지정인증기관(Notified Bodies)에서도 인증을 받을 수 있음

□ 폴란드에 처음 도입되는 전자재는 모두 품질시험을 필하였다는 인증을 받아야 함

---

[22] 폴란드 시험 및 인증 센터 http://www.pcbc.gov.pl/english/

○ 승인서 발급에는 3개월이 소요되며 발급기관은 IBT(Institute for Building Technology)와 그 산하 연구소인 C-BRITI임

□ 폴란드는 EU 위원회의 에너지 라벨링 지침(Council directive/92/75/EEC, 1992)[23]에 의거하여 에너지 효율 등급을 표시하는 에너지 라벨링 제도를 운영하고 있음
  ○ 에너지 소비효율에 따라 등급 라벨 표시 및 최저효율 기준 적용, 에너지 효율 등급, 연간 에너지 소비량 등을 표시함
  ○ 에너지 라벨제도에서 A는 에너지 효율성이 가장 우수한 것을 의미하고 G는 가장 낮은 것을 의미함
  ○ 에너지 라벨 대상 품목은 냉장고, 냉동고, 냉장-냉동고 콤비, 세탁기, 건조기(Electronic tumble dryers), 세탁기-건조기 콤비, 식기 세척기, 램프, 전기 오븐, 에어컨 등으로 대상 품목이 계속 증가하고 있음

□ EU는 관보를 통해 TV에 대한 에너지 라벨 법규(Commission Delegated Regulation No.1062/2010)를 발표하고 11월 30일부터 생산되는 모든 TV에 대해 에너지 라벨 부착을 의무화함

---

[23] http://eur-lex.europa.eu/smartapi/cgi/sga_doc?smartapi!celexplus!prod!celexnumdoc&numdoc=392l0075&lg=en 에서 해당 규정 및 각 나라의 번역본 확인 가능

〈표 Ⅲ-3〉 CE마킹 대상 품목 및 규정 지침

품목	규정지침
가스기기(Appliances Burning Gaseous Fuels)	2009/142/EC
사람 수송용 케이블 (Cableway Installation to Carry Persons)	2000/9/EC
저압 전기 기기 (Low Voltage Electrical Equipment)	2006/95/EC
건설 자재(Construction Products)	89/106/EEC, 93/68/EEC
폭발용 기기 및 보호제품(Equipment and Protective System for used in potentially explosive Atmospheres)	94/9/EC
민간용 폭발물(Explosives for Civil Uses)	93/15/EEC
온수보일러(Hot Water Boiler)	92/42/EEC, 93/68/EEC, 2004/8/EC
승강기(Lift)	95/16/EC
기계(Machinery)	2006/42/EC
선박(Marine Equipment)	96/98/EC
의료기기(Medical Devices)	93/42/EEC, 98/79/EC, 2000/70/EC, 2007/47/EC
의료용 임플란트(Active Implantable Medical Devices)	93/385/EEC, 93/42/EEC, 93/68/EEC, 2007/47/EC
시험관 치료용 기기(In Vitro Diagnostic Medical Devices)	98/79/EC
수동저울(Non-automatic Weighing Instruments)	2009/23/EEC
무선전신 및 통신 단말기기 (Radio Equipment and Telecommunication Terminal Equipment)	99/5/EC
개인보호장비(Personal Protective Equipment)	89/686/EEC, 93/68/EEC, 93/95/EEC, 96/56/EC
단순압력용기(Simple Pressure Vessels)	2009/105/EEC
압력기기(Pressure Equipment)	97/23/EC
여가용보트(Recreational Craft)	94/25/EC
여가용 선박	94/25/EC, 2003/44/EC
장난감(Toys)	88/378/EEC, 93/68/EEC, 2998/48/EC
EMC(Electromagnetic Compatibility)	2004/108/EC
측정기기	2004/22/EC

자료: KOTRA 국가정보

□ 스위스, 독일 등 유럽 9개국이 운영하고 있는 에너지 절약 제품 보급 프로그램인 GEEA(Group for Energy Efficient Appliances)의 에너지 라벨제도 역시 적용되고 있음[24]

□ EU규정 1222/2009에 따라 2012년 6월 이후 제조되어 2012년 11월부터 EU의 시장에 판매되는 타이어는 연비, 소음, 도로밀착 수준을 표시하는 라벨을 스티커로 각 타이어에 부착 혹은 판매장소 표시판에 관련 정보를 표시해야 함

□ 섬유제품과 관련하여 EU가 현행 지침(73/44/EEC, 96/73/EC, 2008/121/EC)을 EU규정(1009/2011 of the European Parliament and of Council, L272, 2011.10.18)으로 바꾸어 시행함으로써 기존 지침들이 무효화됨

□ 식품과 관련하여 영양 성분표 표시가 의무화되었으며 지방, 포화지방, 탄수화물, 당분, 단백질, 염분의 함유량과 열량을 포장 위에 표시해야 함
  ○ 열량과 성분 함유량의 기준은 100g당 또는 100ml당으로 표시되어야 하며 영양 성분표 이외에 추가로 1인분 개당(portion)열량과 성분 함유량을 표시해야 함

□ 소고기, 꿀, 올리브유, 생과일 및 야채 등 일부 식품 및 원산지를 표시하지 않으면 소비자가 오도할 가능성이 있는 그 외 식품은 원산지 라벨을 표시해야 함

□ 혼합식품의 경우 다양한 종류의 고기로 만들어진 육류 식품에는 'formed meat', 다양한 종류의 생선으로 만들어진 생선 식품에는 'formed fish' 라고 표시해야 함

다. 수입 제한 제도[25]

□ 수입허가 품목에 대해서는 대외 경제부의 허가를 취득해야 하며 허가 신청 후 승인

---

[24] KOTRA 국가정보
[25] 한국무역협회 홈페이지 http://www.kita.net

까지는 통상 30일이 소요됨

□ 주류, 담배류, 연료 등의 제품에 대해서는 대외 경제부가 국내 판매 면허를 보유한 기업에 대해 수입쿼터를 할당하거나 일시적으로 수입 금지 조치를 취할 수 있음
  ○ EU 역외 국가에서 수입 시, 주류의 경우 알코올 농도 22%를 넘지 않는 한도 내에서 최대 2리터까지 허가되며 궐련 200개비, 여송연 50개비, 250그램의 담배가 수입 가능함[26]

□ 수입 금지 품목은 유전자 조작식품, 지적재산권 위반제품, 특정국에서 잡히는 참치, 가금류를 제외한 새 등임[27]
  ○ 이 밖에도 중고차(10년 이상 된 승용차 및 6년 이상 된 트럭) 및 2행 정식 엔진을 부착한 운송기구(오토바이)는 수입이 금지됨

□ 수입 감시(Import Monitoring) 품목은 섬유, 의류, 각종 신발류를 비롯해서 철강, 다이아몬드(대상국: 아프리카 국가들) 등이 있음

□ 폴란드에 새로운 제품을 수입할 경우에는 국립보건연구원(National Institute of Hygiene)[28]에 연락을 취해 사전 제품승인을 요청하고 허가를 받아야 함
  ○ 수입자는 요청서와 함께 상업송장 사본, 제품증명서, 생산자의 실험 명세서를 함께 제출해야 함

□ 폴란드에서 외국으로 물품을 수출하는 경우 무기, 위험물질, 쿼터적용 품목 및 특정 원사새, 농산물 등을 수출할 시에는 수출 허가를 취득해야 함
  ○ 수출 허가를 반드시 취득해야 하는 물품은 이 밖에도 철광석, 알루미늄, 원유, 펄프, 면, 모, 주석, 가죽, 고무, 종이 등이 있으며 안전상의 이유로 무기류의 수출은

---

26) Poland Customs, Trade Regulations and Procedures Handbook, 2008
27) 외교통상부, 분야별 통상환경 보고서
28) 폴란드 국립보건원 홈페이지 http://www.pzh.gov.pl/page/?L=1

제한하고 있음

라. 수출입 물품에 부과되는 내국세

1) 관세

☐ 수입 시 납부하는 세금에는 수입 관세(Import Duty), 부가가치세(Value Added Tax), 사치품 판매세(Sale Tax on Luxury Goods), 소비세(Excise Tax) 등이 있음

☐ 폴란드는 EU에 가입한 후 수입하는 물품에 대해서 EU의 공동역외 관세(CET, Common External Tariff)를 부과하고 있음
  ○ EU의 관세는 폴란드에 제품이 수입될 때 CIF(보험료 포함 인도 조건) 상업송장가격을 기준으로 부과됨

☐ EU 가입 이후, 폴란드 공산품의 35%는 수입관세율이 인하, 4%는 인상되었으며, 나머지 61%는 가입 전후 수입관세율 변화가 없었음
  ○ 자동차, 철강 및 철강제품, 시계, 전자제품, 모자, 여행용 가방 등 품목에서 큰 폭의 관세율 인하가 있었음

☐ 농산물의 경우, 수입관세율 인하 및 인상 품목은 비슷한 비율이며 27%의 품목에는 변화가 없었음
  ○ 담배, 와인, 말린 과일, 향신료 등의 관세율 인하 폭이 컸으며 바나나, 레몬, 포도, 등 일부 과일과 우유, 치즈 등 유제품 및 쌀은 수입관세율 인상 폭이 컸음

☐ EU 집행위가 관세율을 규정하기 위해 위원회 규정 No. 1006/2011[29]을 통해 WCO HS 협약 개정안을 반영한 복합품목분류표(CN: Combined Nomenclature)를 발표하였으며

---

29) http://eur-lex.europa.eu/LexUriServ/LexUriServ.do?uri=OJ:L:2011:282:0001:0912:EN:PDF에서 확인

새로운 복합품목분류표는 2012년 1월 1일부터 시행됨
  ○ HS 6단위까지는 협약 개정안과 동일하고, 추가적으로 8단위까지 운영하며 기본 관세율을 규정하고 있음

□ 폴란드에 수입하는 제품에 부과되는 관세 및 기타 세금은 공식 관세 브라우저 ISZTAR 외에 TARIC (EU집행위 관세 사이트)에 접속하여 확인할 수 있음[30]
  ○ TARIC은 매일 업데이트되며 제품의 원산지, HS코드 혹은 집행위원회 총국 웹사이트에 게재된 제품의 설명을 통해 제품에 부과되는 관세 및 세금을 검색할 수 있음
  ○ TARIC 관세 사이트의 관세율 확인은 http://ec.europa.eu/taxation_customs/dds2/taric/taric_consultation.jsp?Lang=en → Good Code 란에 HS번호 6자리 입력 → Country of Origin/Destination에서 해당 국가 클릭 → Retrieve Measures 클릭 → 해당 국가별 품목에 대한 관세율을 확인할 수 있음

□ EU는 GATT(현 WTO)가입국뿐만 아니라 비가입국에도 협정 관세를 부과하는 것을 원칙으로 하나 관세동맹 체결 여부에 따라 일방 또는 쌍무특혜 관세 조치를 취함

□ 일반적으로 적용되는 관세율은 종가관세(Advalorem Tariff)이며 석탄, 농산물 일부, 식품, 영화 필름 등에는 종량세(Specific Duties), 담배, 과일, 카페트 및 시계 등에는 선택 관세(Alternative Tariff)가 적용됨

□ 과일, 채소, 화훼류 등의 상품에는 계절관세(Seasonal Tariff)가 적용되며 농산물에 대해서는 수입부과금(Import Levy)이 함께 부과됨

2) 한·EU FTA 관세 양허

□ 한국과 EU는 FTA 발효 후 5년 내 한국이 10,538개 항목의 관세를, EU가 9,803개 항목의 관세를 100% 철폐하기로 합의함

---

30) http://www.ttb.gov/itd/poland.shtml#REQUIREMENTS

□ 품목 기준으로 EU는 모든 품목의 관세를 5년 내 철폐하며 한국은 의료용 전자기기, 건설 중장비, 순모직물, 합판 등의 품목에 대해 7년간의 철폐구간을 두기로 합의함

〈표 Ⅲ-1〉 한·EU FTA 상품 양허 결과

(단위: 개, %, 억달러)

양허유형	한국 양허				EU 양허			
	품목수	비중	對EU 수입액	비중	품목수	비중	對한국 수입액	비중
즉시(A)	9,195	81.7	182	66.7	9,252	94.0	318	76.6
2-3년(B)	625	5.5	61	22.2	282	2.9	69	16.7
5년(C)	718	6.4	22	8.1	269	2.7	28	6.7
6-7년	10,538	93.6	265	97.0	9,803	99.6	415	100
10년	111	1.0	4	1.4				
10년 초과	399	3.5	3	1.1				
양허제외/ 현행관세	169	1.5	1	0.5				
총합계	44	0.4	0	0.0	39	0.4	0	0.0
	11,261	100	273	100	9,842	100	415	100

주: 품목 수는 HS2006기준 금액은 2004~2006년 평균 기준임
   농업세이프가드, 수입쿼터, 시장진입가격제도 등은 관세철폐연도에 따라 분류
자료: 한·EU FTA 설명자료, 외교통상부

□ 우리나라 주 수출 품목인 자동차 관세에 대해 양측은 배기량 크기별로 동일한 양허안 구조에 합의함
  ○ 중형과 대형(배기량 1500cc 초과)차량에 대한 관세는 협정 발효 후 3년 내, 소형(배기량 1500cc 이하)에 대한 관세는 5년 내 철폐함[31]
  ○ 가솔린 자동차용 엔진, 기어박스 등 주요 자동차 부품에 대한 관세 역시 양측 모두 즉시 철폐함

□ 전기전자 관련 EU측의 고관세 품목의 관세가 5년 내에 철폐되며 전기전자부품의 모든 관세를 즉시 철폐함

---

31) 기획재정부, 「FTA활용 핸드북」 83면

〈표 Ⅲ-2〉 한·EU FTA양허 단계별 주요 품목

한국 양허		EU 양허	
품목 수 기준 95.8% 3년 내 철폐 일부 민감 품목에 대해 7년 철폐 확보		품목 수 기준 99.4% 3년 내 철폐 전 품목 관세를 5년 내 철폐	
즉시	자동차 부품, 컬러TV	즉시	자동차 부품, 무선통신기기부품, 에어컨 등
3년	중대형 승용차, 의약품, 무선 통신기기 부품 등	3년	중대형 승용차, 타이어, 합성수지 등
5년	소형 승용차, 기초화장품, 의료용 전자기기 등	5년	소형 승용차, 컬러 TV, 영상기록 재생 용기 등
7년	순모직물, 합판, 건설 중장비 등		

자료: 외교통상부, 2008, 한·EU FTA 상세 설명자료

□ 보다 자세한 관세 양허 품목과 양허율에 대한 정보는 한·EU FTA 포털사이트32)에 접속하여 협정문을 참고하면 알 수 있음

3) 부가가치세

□ 폴란드 부가가치세는 1993년 처음 도입되었으며 2004년 5월 1일부터 EU세법에 의거하여 VAT를 규정하고 있음

□ 2011년 1월부터 부가가치세 세율이 인상되어 기본 세율은 23%이며 대부분의 물품과 서비스 판매에 부과되나 일부 제품이나 서비스에는 부가세율이 인하되어 (deducted VAT rate)과세됨33)

□ EU 역내 물품이나 국제 운송 서비스, 서적, 항공기 부품의 경우 부가가치세가 부여되지 않으며 일부 식품이나 아동용품, 보건 제품, 호텔 서비스, 수송 서비스 등의 경우 8%의 세율을 적용함

---

32) http://www.fta.go.kr/eu
33) 폴란드 투자유치청 홈페이지 http://www.paiz.gov.pl/polish_law/taxation

〈표 Ⅲ-3〉 물품 및 서비스별 부가세율 현황

(단위: %)

변경 전 세율	변경 후 세율	물품 및 서비스
22	23	기본세율 - 대부분 품목에 적용
7	8	일부식품, 약품 및 보건 관련 제품, 비료, 일부 아동용품, 호텔 및 케이터링(catering)서비스, 일부 수송 서비스, 도시 서비스(상수, 하수처리, 도로 유지 등)
3	5	책, 잡지 및 기본 식품
면세	0	EU 역내 물품 공급, 일부 국제 운송 서비스 및 관련 서비스, 서적 및 특정 잡지, 선박 및 항공기용 일부 물품
		금융용역, 교육용역, 보건용역, 문화관련 용역

자료: How to business, 폴란드 투자 유치청

□ 일부 금융 및 보험 서비스, 문화 서비스, 연구개발 등 부가세가 면제되는 분야에 있어서 납세 기업은 매입부가가치세(input VAT)를 환급받을 수 없음
  ○ 부가세 납부 업체 사이의 거래는 부가세 상업송장(Faktura VAT invoice)으로 처리해야 함

□ 등록된 부가세 납부업체는 매월 부가세 신고서를 관할 세무서에 제출해야 하고 부가세 관련 구매 및 판매 기록을 유지해야 함

4) 소비세[34]

□ 소비세는 EU 소비세법과 일치하는 과세대상과 일치하지 않는 과세대상 두 가지로 나누어짐
  ○ EU 소비세법과 일치하는 과세대상은 자동차, 연료, 가스, 알코올음료, 담배 등이며 일치하지 않는 과세대상은 여객자동차, 화장품, 모피, 총기류 등임
  ○ 소비세는 폴란드에서 제조하는 과세대상 물건, 창고에서 물품의 반출, 공급 및 과세 대상 물건의 수입, EU 역내 국가 간의 공급 및 취득, 과세대상 물건의 교환 및 무상 공급에 대하여도 과세됨

---

[34] 국세청, 「폴란드 진출기업을 위한 세무안내」, 2010

□ 과세대상 물건을 수출하는 경우 특별소비세는 면제되나 특별소비세가 과세되지 않은 물건을 취득 및 소유하는 경우에는 특별소비세가 부과됨

□ 소비세의 과세기간은 1개월이며 신고는 당월분 실적에 대하여 다음달 25일까지 신고하여야 함
  ○ EU 특별소비세법과 일치하는 과세대상은 매일 선납이 이루어져야 하며 익월 25일 신고 시 선납 분을 반영하여 신고서를 제출해야 함
  ○ 수입재화에 대한 특별소비세는 관세의 납부절차와 같음

5) 수입 규제를 위한 과세

□ EU가 한국산 제품에 부과하고 있는 반덤핑관세(컬러TV, 컬러 브라운관 등), 세이프가드(철강제품), 상계관세(반도체) 등의 수입규제조치는 폴란드 수출 시 그대로 적용되었으나 현재 대부분의 규제가 종료됨

□ EU는 2012년 2월 9일자 관보를 통하여 한국, 모로코, 몰도바 등을 경유하여 수입되는 강철 로프 및 케이블에 대해 원산지가 어디든지 간에 확정적 반덤핑관세를 확대 적용한다는 내용의 2012년 1월 27일자 시의회 시행규정(EU) 102/2012[35])을 게재하였음
  ○ 반덤핑관세율은 한국 및 모로코를 경유하는 수입에 대해서는 종전과 같이 60.4%의 관세율을 유지하며 반덤핑관세 부과가 면제되었던 한국의 11개 업체에 대해서도 계속 관세 부과를 면제하기로 결정함
  ○ 확정적 반덤핑 관세 부과조치가 연장된 제품은 로크드 코일로프를 포함한 강철로프 및 케이블로서 최대 직경 3mm를 초과하는 것임

□ EU 집행위는 2012년 2월 28일로 한국산 폴리에틸렌텔레프탈레이트(polyethyleneterephthalate, PET)에 대한 반덤핑 조치를 종료한다는 통지를 공표하였음[36])

---

35) http://eur-lex.europa.eu/LexUriServ/LexUriServ.do?uri=OJ:L:2012:036:0001:0016:EN:PDF 참조
36) http://eurlex.europa.eu/LexUriServ/LexUriServ.do?Uri=O J:C:2012:057:0010:0010:EN:PDF 참조

○ EU 집행위는 이와 관련하여 반덤핑 조치를 연장해야 한다는 특별한 요청이 없었다고 밝혔음
○ 이에 따라 지난 한국산 PET의 對EU 수입은 2007년 이후 이사회 규정 192-2007에 의거한 반덤핑 조치를 적용받지 않게 되었음

☐ EU는 1년에 상·하반기 2차례에 걸쳐 역내 공급이 수요를 못 따라가거나 일시적으로 수요가 급증하여 EU 역내 생산만으로 수요를 충족시킬 수 없는 품목에 대해 일시적으로 관세를 면제해주고 있음
○ 해당하는 관세 면제 품목은 EU 관보를 통해서 발표되며 EU 관보는 EU 집행위 사이트[37])에서 확인할 수 있음[38])

〈표 Ⅲ-4〉 EU 반덤핑 및 상계관세 규제 정보

No.	규제국	한국 HS CODE	품목명	규제내용	조사개시일
1	유럽연합	732110	철강 로프 및 케이블 (Steel Ropes and Cables)	AD (규제중)	2012.02.10
2	유럽연합	540220	폴리에스터 고강력사 (High tenacity yarn of Polyesters)	AD (규제종료)	2009.09.08
3	유럽연합	7219.31.0000, 32.1000, 9000, 33.1000, 9000, 34.1000, 9000, 35.1000, 9000, 7220.20	스테인레스 냉연강판(Flat-rolled products of stainless steel, not further worked than cold-rolled(cold-reduced))	AD (규제종료)	2008.02.01
4	유럽연합	854011	컬러TV용 브라운관(CPT, Cathode-ray Color Television Picture Tubes)	AD (규제종료)	2006.01.11

---

37) http://europa.eu/newsroom/press-releases/index_en.htm
38) 한국무역협회 블로그 http://blog.naver.com/kitablog

〈표 Ⅲ-4〉의 계속

No.	규제국	한국 HS CODE	품목명	규제내용	조사개시일
5	유럽연합	8418.1	양문형 냉장고 (Side by Side Refrigerator)	AD (규제종료)	2005.06.02
6	유럽연합	8542.21.2010	DRAM(Dynamic Random Access Memory) - 모든 유형의 DRAM과 densities 및 파생품	CVD (규제종료)	2002.07.25
7	유럽연합	7307.93, 7307.99	철강제 관연결구류 (tube and pipe fitting of iron or steel)	AD (규제중)	2001.06.01
8	유럽연합	3920.62.00.00	PET Film(Film of Polyethylene Terephthalate, * 탄력성 마그네틱 디스크와 광중합 프린팅 플레이트 관련 필름은 제외)	AD (규제종료)	2000.05.27
9	유럽연합	3907.6	PET CHIP (※플라스틱 병을 만드는데 쓰이는 중간재) - 페트병, 페트필름, 폴리에스텔 제조원료	AD (규제종료)	1999.11.06
10	유럽연합	5503.20.1000, 9000	폴리에스터 합성단섬유(Synthetic fibers of polyesters) - 쿠션, 자동차 시트, 자켓 등의 섬유제품의 기초재료	AD (규제종료)	1999.10.07
11	유럽연합	8528-12-9010, 9020, 9030, 9040, 9050, 9060	컬러 TV (17 " 이하 및 18 " 이상)	AD (규제종료)	1988.02.17

자료: 한국무역협회 수입규제 정보 사이트 http://antidumping.kita.net/

□ EU가입 직전까지 폴란드는 한국과 관련하여 4건의 세이프가드(Calcium Carbide, Gas Water Heaters, Matches, Certain Steel Products)가 실행되고 있었으나 2004년 4월 30일자로 모두 효력이 상실됨

□ EU는 원칙적으로 수입 쿼터 제도를 적용하지 않고 있으며 WTO협정 내에서 2004년까지 일부 섬유제품에 대한 쿼터 제도가 적용되었으나 2005년 1월 1일부로 전부 폐지됨

6) 통관사 수수료 및 운송비용

☐ 40feet 컨테이너 물량의 door to door 이삿짐 운송의 경우 폴란드에서 한국까지 약 7,000유로를 지불해야 하며 내륙운송, 환적 등 부대조건으로 인해 총운송비가 EU 국가 중 비싼 편에 속함

☐ 상품 운송의 경우 물량과 운송 거리에 따라 운송비의 차이가 상당히 크며 20feet 컨테이너 상품 운송의 경우 폴란드에서 한국까지 해운 운송비는 약 3,000~4,000유로임

☐ 2011년 7월 1일부터 폴란드 내 도로이용 요금이 개편되어 기존에 3,500PLN에서 1km당 35grosz로 화물차량 운전자에 부과되고 있음[39]

7) 일반특혜 관세 제도(GSP)

☐ 개도국의 수출 확대와 산업화를 촉진하기 위해 개도국의 제품에 대해 낮은 수입 관세율을 적용하는 제도로서 현재 176개국에 혜택을 제공하고 있으나 한국은 EU의 GSP혜택에서 제외됨
  ○ GSP+제도는 표준 GSP제도에 추가하여 노동권 보호를 포함한 지속가능한 개발을 추진하는 국가에 대해 추가적으로 혜택을 더 제공하는 것임

마. 관세의 감면·면제·유예제도

1) 면세구역(DFZ)[40]

☐ 면세구역(DFZ)에서는 EU 또는 EEA외 국가에서 수입된 외국상품이 수입관세, 소비

---

[39] 관련 내용 및 비용 산정에 관한 규정사항은 http://www.emapa.pl/Toll_in_Poland에서 확인할 수 있음
[40] 투자안내서-폴란드 비즈니스 가이드 http://paiz.gov.pl /www.jpweber.com

세 및 VAT 없이 판매됨
- ○ 사람이 주거하지 않는 독립된 구역이며 관세제도가 예외없이 적용되는 외국지역으로 취급됨
- ○ DFZ의 모든 입구 및 출구는 세관의 감독하에 있으며 모든 제품의 반출 또한 세관에서 감독함
- ○ 폴란드에는 현재 그다인스크항구, 시비노우이시치에, 슈체친, 테레스폴, 바르샤바공항, 모슈초누프, 글리비체 총 7곳의 면세구역이 있음

2) 보세창고 제도[41]

□ 보세창고는 EU 혹은 EEA 외 국가에서 수입된 관세과세물품이 보관된 기타 안전지역으로서 물품 수입과 관련된 모든 지불(수입관세, 소비세 및 VAT)이 폴란드 내 소비가 이루어질 때까지 연기됨
- ○ 관세 과세물품은 계약하에 지불조건이나 관세 없이 제조되었거나 혹은 제조과정에 있는 혹은 수입업자나 그 대행사 및 세관원이 공동으로 보관하고 있는 물건을 말함
- ○ 폴란드에는 현재 그다인스크항구, 시비노우이시치에, 슈체친, 테레스폴, 바르샤바공항, 모슈초누프, 글리비체 등 총 7곳의 면세구역에 보세창고가 있음
- ○ 보세지역에서의 모든 행위에 대해서는 관세, 쿼터, 수입제한 등의 적용을 받지 않음

3) 외국기업에 대한 부가가치세 환급[42]

□ 2010년 1월 1일부터 비거주자인 외국기업도 부가가치세 환급을 받을 수 있게 되었으며 외국기업이 EU 회원국이 아닌 경우에는 상호주의에 의하여 환급이 적용됨
- ○ 환급을 신청하는 외국기업은 폴란드의 부가가치세 등록 사업자가 아니거나 폴란드 영토 내에서 사업을 영위하고 있지 않아야 하고 그 기업이 거주하거나 고정 사

---

[41] 투자안내서-폴란드 비즈니스 가이드 http://paiz.gov.pl /www.jpweber.com
[42] 폴란드 투자 유치청 홈페이지 http://www.paiz.gov.pl/polish_law/taxation/vat

업장이 위치해 있는 국가의 부가가치세 등록 사업자여야 함

☐ 환급 신청을 위해서는 폴란드어로 작성된 신청서와 부가가치세 상업송장 원본 또는 통관서류 원본, 부가가치세 환급 신청자가 자신의 거주지국의 부가가치세 과세 사업자라는 증명서를 제출해야 함
  ○ 부가가치세 과세사업자라는 증명서는 부가가치세 환급 신청자가 거주하는 국가의 행정기관이 발행한 것이어야 하며 폴란드 재무부 규정에서 정하는 서식과 일치해야 함
  ○ 만일 증명서가 폴란드 재무부 규정에 정하는 서식과 일치하지 않는다면 폴란드 재무부 규정이 정하는 서식이 요구하는 정보를 모두 담고 있어야 함

☐ 3개월 이상 1년 이하의 기간에 대한 환급을 다음해 9월 30일까지 신청해야 하며 환급은 신청 후 4개월 이내에 이루어지나 서류에 대한 세밀한 확인이 필요하다면 기간은 늘어날 수 있음
  ○ 환급은 폴란드화로 환급 신청기업의 계좌에 입금되며 환급계좌가 외국계좌일 경우 송금비용은 환급 신청자가 부담해야 함

2. 수출국의 수입준비(FTA 수출통관 준비 절차)

가. 품목 번호 및 관세 혜택 확인

☐ 한 · EU FTA가 비준되었기 때문에 한국에서 EU 국가인 폴란드로 수출할 경우 FTA 수출통관 준비 절차를 따라야 함
  ○ FTA 수출통관 준비 절차는 ① FTA 협정 발효국 여부 확인하기 → ② 품목번호 확인하기 → ③ FTA 관세혜택 확인하기 → ④ 원산지 결정기준 확인하기 → ⑤ 원산지 증명서 발급하기 → ⑥ 수출 및 관련 서류 보관하기의 순서임

□ FTA 특혜관세를 받기 위한 품목번호를 확인하는 방법에는 유권해석을 받는 법과 직접 확인하는 법이 있으며 직접 확인 시 인터넷(관세청 인터넷 통관 포탈), 전화(국내 1577-8577/해외 02-3438-5199) 혹은 각 지역 세관에 방문하여 확인할 수 있음

□ 유권해석을 받을 시에는 수출신고 전에 '품목분류 사전심사제도'를 이용하고 수출실적이 있는 경우 '품목번호 확인서'를 받으면 됨
  ○ 품목분류 사전심사제도는 수출신고는 수출자 및 관세사, 관세법인 또는 통관 취급법인이 신청서를 작성해 인터넷, 우편 또는 방문 등으로 신청함
    - 관세행정전자통관시스템(UNI-PASS) → 민원사무검색(품목분류 사전심사신청) 또는 업무처리(기타 전자민원 → 품목분류 사전심사신청)의 단계임
  ○ 품목분류 사전심사제도는 신청 후 보정기간 및 분석기간을 제외하고 약 15일이 소요됨

□ 품목번호 확인서는 HS품목번호 확인 신청서 및 첨부서류(신청 대상상품의 견본, 견본 제출이 곤란한 경우 사유서 및 사진, 제조회사의 성분표시, 제조사양 설명서, 상품 설명서 등)를 준비하여 신고한 세관에 우편 또는 방문 접수로 신청하면 됨
  ○ 품목번호 확인서 발급에는 15일 미만의 기간이 소요되며 제출된 자료의 보완 기간은 제외됨

□ 품목별 협정에 따른 세율은 관세청 홈페이지[43])에서 확인할 수 있으며 일반세율과 특혜관세율 중 유리한 것을 선택할 수 있음
  ○ 협정세율 적용 신청을 위해서는 증명서 발급기관, 원산지 결정 기준 등을 확인한 후 원산지 승빙서를 근거로 '협정관세 적용신청서'를 작성해 세관에 제출해야 함

나. 원산지 증명

□ 대한민국 또는 EU를 원산지로 하는 상품에 대해 관세혜택이 부여되므로 한·EU

---

43) http://fta.customs.go.kr/kcsweb/template/html/fta2010/html/kor/main/hsgod/DBAQ638.html

FTA에서 정한 원산지 결정기준(원산지 제품의 정의 및 행정협력의 방법에 관한 의정서)을 충족해야 함
- ○ 한 · EU FTA는 완전생산기준, 세번 변경기준, 부가가치 기준(MC 40~50%, 계산법의 경우 직접법, 제품가격기준은 공장도 기준), 가공공정기준을 적용함[44]
- ○ 제품별 원산지 결정기준은 FTA 포털사이트[45]에서 품목이나 HS Code를 입력한 후 확인할 수 있음

□ 특혜관세를 적용받기 위한 원산지 인증서 발급 절차를 간소화하기 위해 한국과 EU는 2010년 4월부터 각국의 관세청에서 인증 수출자로 지정받을 수 있는 '원산지 인증 수출자 제도'를 도입함[46]
- ○ 원산지 증명 능력이 있다고 인증된 수출자에는 원산지 증명서 발급 절차 또는 첨부서류 제출 간소화 혜택을 부여함
- ○ 지정된 원산지 증명서 양식은 없으며 Invoice Declaration 양식에 '원산지 신고서' 문안을 기재해야 함
- ○ 인증번호체계는 국가명(2자리), 세관번호(6자리), 일련번호(4자리) 등으로 구성되며 폴란드의 경우 국가명은 PL로 표기함
- ○ 원산지 인증 수출자로 인증받기 위해 소요되는 기간은 최소 4~8주 정도로 예상할 수 있음

□ 한국 기업이 EU지역으로 건당 6,000유로(약 950만원) 초과 물품을 수출하고자 할 때 관세청에서 인증 수출자로 지정된 기업만이 원산지 인증서를 자율 발급해 특혜관세를 적용받을 수 있음
- ○ 건당 6,000유로 이하의 물품 수출 기업의 경우는 인증 수출자 지정을 받지 않아도 원산지 증명서를 자율 발급하여 수출할 수 있음
- ○ 인증 수출자의 지정은 서울, 부산, 인천, 대구, 광주 다섯 곳의 세관에서 가능함

---

44) http://fta.customs.go.kr/kcsweb/template/html/fta2010/html/kor/main/hsgod/DBAQ638.html
45) http://fta.customs.go.kr/kcsweb/template/html/fta2010/html/kor/main/hsgod/DBAQ638.html
46) 관계부처합동 자료, 「한 · EU FTA로 달라지는 우리 생활」

□ 원산지 검증의 경우 간접검증 및 공동검증제도를 채택하여 수입국 관련 공무원은 수출국 관세당국의 동의를 얻고 원산지 검증에 참석할 수 있게 되었음
  ○ 원칙적으로는 수입국 관세당국이 수출국 관세당국에 원산지 요건 충족 여부를 확인요청해야 하며 간접검증을 보완하기 위해 공동 검증을 실시함
  ○ 수입국 관세당국이 무작위 혹은 합리적 의심에 기초하여 수출국 관세당국에 검증을 요구하였을 때 수출국 관세당국이 검증 결과를 수입국에 통보함으로써 검증을 완료할 수 있음
  ○ 단, 10개월 내 수출국의 관세당국이 수입국의 요청에 미회신 시 수입국에서는 협정관세 적용을 배제할 수 있음

□ 원산지 증명과 관련하여 폴란드 세관이 2010년 한국의 전자인증 원산지 증명서를 수용하기로 결정함에 따라 원산지 증명서의 전자인증 문제로 인한 통관 장애가 해소됨
  ○ 폴란드 재무부는 한국의 전자인증 원산지 증명서에 대해 직접 직인, 서명할 것을 요구하였던 기존의 방식을 철회하고 전국의 지방세관에 한국의 전자인증 원산지 증명서를 수용토록 지시함

□ 원산지 증명서에 대한 정확성은 사후에 검증하는 것을 원칙으로 하기 때문에 자료 보관 의무가 있으며(한·EU FTA 경우 5년) 이를 위반할 경우 특혜관세 적용을 배제함

〈표 Ⅲ-5〉 원산지 증명 보관 서류

보관주체	수입자	수출자	생산자
보관서류	- 원산시 증명시 사본 - 수입거래계약서 - 수입물품 운송서류	- 원산지증명서 사본 - 원산지통보서 - 원산지 증명서 발급 신청 서류 사본 - 수출품 출납 서류 - 수출품 구매 계약서	- 원산지 통보서 사본 - 수출물품 및 재료 생산, 구매, 출납 서류 - 공정명세서 - 원가계산서 - 수출품 공급 계약서

자료: FTA 포털사이트 http://fta.customs.go.kr/

3. 수입통관 절차

□ 수입통관 절차는 크게 ①물품 도착 전 준비→②물품 반입 및 검사→③세금 납부 및 반출→④관세 환급의 4단계로 분류할 수 있음

□ 폴란드는 EU 가입 이후 세관행정 대부분을 전산화함에 따라 통관 관련 문제는 감소하고 있으나 불법적인 행위 적발과 검사 등에 중점을 두어 통관 절차가 다소 꼼꼼하게 진행되고 있음
　ㅇ EU 법규에 따라 기업은 EU 역내에서 통관할 국가를 선택할 수 있는데 다수의 외국 기업들이 통관지를 독일 및 네덜란드 등으로 옮겨가고 있음

가. 물품 도착 전 준비

□ 2010년 12월 31부터 한국에서 EU로 수출하는 화물의 운송인은 화물 적재 24시간 전에 최초 도착항 관할 세관에 도착신고서(ENS, Entry Summary Declaration)[47] 제출 의무가 있음
　ㅇ 운송 수단 및 운송 시간에 따라 세관에 ENS를 제출하는 시한이 다양하므로 운송인은 미리 통보 시한을 참고하여 ENS의 제출시기를 맞추도록 해야 함
　ㅇ 수입물품 운송인 및 대리인, 통관 절차 이행 대리인, 보세구역 운영인, 도착보고 생략대상 물품, 우편물, 여행용품 및 기타 상업적 가치가 낮은 물품의 운송인 및 대리인은 보세구역 반입 즉시 도착 신고서 작성 및 제출 의무가 있음
　ㅇ 추가적으로 도착신고서를 제출할 때 소요되는 비용은 약 25달러임

□ 전기에너지, 파이프를 통해 반입되는 화물, 우편 서신 및 소포, 여행객의 수화물이 포함된 화물 등 구두 신고가 허용된 화물의 경우에는 ENS신고가 면제됨

---

[47] http://ec.europa.eu/ecip/documents/procedures/import_faq_en.pdf에서 자세한 지침 확인

〈표 Ⅲ-6〉 운송 수단에 따른 ENS 제출 시기

구분	세관 통보시한
컨테이너 해상화물(단거리 제외)	출발지에서 선적 개시 24시간 전
벌크화물(단거리 제외)	EU영역 최초 항구 도착 4시간 전
단거리 해상화물	EU영역 최초 항구 도착 2시간 전
단거리 비행(4시간 이내)	비행기 실제 이륙시간까지
장거리 비행(4시간 초과)	비행기가 EU영역 최초 공항 도착 4시간 전
철도/운하	EU영역 내의 세관 도착 2시간 전
육로	EU영역 내의 세관 도착 1시간 전

자료: 유럽위원회 홈페이지(http://ec.europa.eu/ecip/security_amendment/procedures/index_en.htm)

□ 폴란드의 주요 무역항은 GDANSK, GDYNIA, SZCZECIN이며 한국·폴란드 간 항해 일수는 약 7주(약 40~50일)가 소요됨

□ 폴란드 내 공항은 총 12개이며 (Bydgoszcz, Gdansk, Katowice, Krakow, Lodz, Poznan, Rzeszow, Szczecin, Warszawa, Wroclaw, Zielona Gora, 등) 수도인 바르샤바 공항은 Warsaw Frederic Chopin Airport임[48]

□ 수입신고는 소정의 공정양식(SAD, Single Administrative Document)[49] 및 상업송장, 포장명세표 등의 구비서류를 첨부하여야 하며 수입물품의 화주 또는 그 대리인으로서 관세청에 등록된 관세사, 통관법인, 관세사법인의 명으로만 가능함
  ○ 수입신고서와 함께 상업송장, 가격신고서(발송별 물품 가치가 10,000유로 이상의 경우), 원산지 증명서, B/L(선하증권)부본 또는 AWB(항공화물운송장)부본이 필요함
  ○ 산 동물이나 고기 또는 육류 식품 등의 경우에는 검역 증명서, 식물과 과일의 경우 식물 병리학 증명서, 핵 제품과 폭발물의 경우에는 폐기물 처리 또는 운송 허가증

---

[48] www.lotnisko-chopina.pl에서 항공 운항 정보를 얻을 수 있음
[49] SAD 관련 규정 및 양식은 http://ec.europa.eu/taxation_customs/customs/procedural_aspects/general/sad/index_en.htm에서 찾을 수 있음

이 필요함
- ○ 보호대상이 야생동물이나 식물의 경우에는 수입허가나 CITES 증명서 등을 첨부해야 함

□ 수입 신고 시 수출자의 상호와 주소(우편번호 포함), 선적 물품의 상세설명, HS code(적어도 6자리), 위험물일 경우 UN code[50]가 분명하게 표기되어 있어야 함

나. 물품의 반입 및 검사

□ 보세구역(세관 지정 세관 사무소, 세관 지정 혹은 세관이 승인한 기타 장소, 자유지역)에서의 물품 반출 검사 및 샘플 채취 등은 세관이 허가한 대상에 한하여 가능함

□ 수입물품 하역 및 환적은 원칙적으로 세관 허가 대상이며 긴급 사유 등 예외적 경우에 한해 세관은 즉시 통지 후 수입 물품의 하역 및 환적이 가능함
- ○ 검사, 샘플채취 및 운송 수단 검사 목적으로 세관은 수입물품의 하역 및 포장 개봉 요구를 할 수 있음
- ○ 물품의 동일성 검사 및 필요 시 견본검사가 이루어지며 비용은 세관이 부담함

□ 신고인은 물품검사에 따른 제반사항에 협조해야 하고 또한 관련 비용을 부담해야 하며 검사 및 견본 검사 시 입회권을 가짐

□ 물품검사는 일반적으로 세관이 정한 시간에 세관 통제 구역인 부두, 창고 등 지정된 장소에서 이루어짐
- ○ 세관이 지정한 장소에서 검사가 곤란한 플랜트 설비, 정밀기기, 귀중품, 긴급수요 물자, door to door로 운반되는 물품의 경우 세관원이 현장에서 직접 검사함
- ○ 세관은 필요할 경우 미리 제출된 수입신고서 관련 서류를 검증하거나 추가 자료

---

50) 유엔 위험품 운송전문가 위원회(UN Committee of Experts on the Transport of Dangerous Good) 에서, 특정 위험품을 구별하기 위하여 부여한 4자리로 구성된 단위 부호

제출을 요구할 수 있으며 수입물품의 샘플을 채취할 수 있음
  ○ 물품의 동일성 검사 및 필요 시 견본검사가 이루어지며 비용은 세관이 부담함

다. 세금 납부 후 화물 출고

□ 일반적으로 관세, 특별세, 부가가치세는 통관 시 지불하며 관세 등의 포탈이 확인될 경우 해당 금액과 이자(통관서류 제출일 기준으로 계산)를 7일 이내에 세관에 납부해야함

□ 수입신고 수리 및 관세 납부(담보제공)가 이루어진 물품은 원칙적으로 보세구역에서 즉시 반출 가능함
  ○ 정해진 기간 내에 수입물품 검사를 수행하지 못한 경우 혹은 납부 기한 내에 관세 납부 또는 보증이 이루어지지 못한 경우에는 반출이 불가능함
  ○ 수입관세가 일부 면제되는 일시적 수입절차에는 적용을 배제함
  ○ 제한 또는 금지품목에 해당하는 물품이 아닌 경우 세관은 신고서의 항목이 확인되거나 혹은 확인될 필요가 없을 시 접수 직후 바로 통관함

□ 자유유통을 위해 통관된 물품이 통관신고의 하자 등을 이유로 통관 무효가 되거나 역내 가공절차하의 관세 환급, 하자 및 위약물품에 대한 관세 환급 혹은 환불 시 역내 물품의 지위를 상실하게 됨

라. 간이 절차(Simplified Procedure)

□ 통관업무의 적정성을 유지하는 범위 내에서 통관 형식과 절차의 간소화를 위해 EU는 간이통관 제도를 설치, 운영하고 있음
  ○ 간이신고방식은 정식 제출서류를 면제하거나 기타 공용 또는 상용서류로 대행하는 것임
  ○ 기장 방식의 경우 수입자가 물품의 세관 제출을 생략하고 자사의 사업장으로 직

접 반입, 자신의 장부에 기재 후 세관에 추후 통보하여도 통관 신고서 제출과 동등한 법적 효력을 지닐 수 있음

☐ 신고인은 일반적, 주기적 성격의 사후보충신고서를 작성하여 세관에 제출해야 함
  ○ 보충신고서는 간이신고서가 접수된 날로부터 효력을 발생하는 단일 불가분의 문서로 간주됨

마. 수출 통관 절차

☐ 수출신고는 서류신고(SAD) 및 전자신고 모두 가능하고 구비서류는 상업송장, 선하증권, 적하목록 등 이며 필요 시 원산지 증명서를 구비해야 함

☐ 폴란드의 일반적인 수출통관 절차는 ① VAT금액을 제외시킨 수출 상업송장 발행 → ② 운송 트럭 혹은 제품박스에 Seal 부착 → ③ ECS(Export Control System) 신고 준비 → ④ 세관에서 IE529 전자 메세지 발행(수출 가능) → ⑤ 수출 확정 처리 → ⑥ EU 외 지역으로 물건 발송 → ⑦ 세관에서 IE599 전자 메세지 발행(수출 완료)의 과정으로 이루어짐

☐ 현재 EU는 수출관세를 적용하지 않고 있으며 EU 국경세관에서 운송 트럭이 국경을 넘었을 때 발행하는 IE599 전자 메세지와 관련한 수수료 또한 없음

☐ 현재 EU는 원칙적으로 수출 시 VAT를 면제하고 있으나 관할 세관에 수출 완료 사실을 알리지 않았을 경우 혹은 수출이 제대로 완료되지 않았을 경우에는 VAT를 지불해야 함

☐ 무기, 위험물질, 쿼터적용 품목 및 특정 원자재, 농산물 등을 비롯하여 문화상품과 이중 용도 품목 수출의 경우에는 수출허가를 취득해야 함

바. 관세 등의 환급[51]

☐ EU는 역외로부터 수입한 물품으로 제조한 물품을 역외로 수출하는 경우 수입원재료에 대한 관세를 환급 혹은 감면해주는 역내가공구제조치(Inward Processing Relief) 제도를 운영하고 있음
  ○ 한·EU FTA협상의 쟁점이었던 관세 환급은 현행 제도를 유지하되 협정 발표 5년 후부터 특정 요건을 충족할 경우 해당 품목에 대한 관세 환급 한도를 제한하는 세이프가드 조치를 도입하기로 함

☐ 폴란드에서 관세 환급은 수입된 물품이 수출용 원부자재인 경우 SAD를 받아 신청서 작성 후 세관당국으로부터 환급을 받을 수 있음
  ○ 수출용 원부자재에 대한 SAD를 받는 데는 보통 7일에서 14일이 소요되며 관세 환급 신청이 타당하다고 인정될 시 바로 환급이 이루어짐

☐ 관세의 환급 절차는 ① 물품 수입(무상 제공품을 만들 시에는 관세를 납부해야 함) → ② 가공 처리 → ③ 물품의 재수출 → ④ 수출품에 대한 관세 환급의 과정으로 이루어짐

☐ 관세 환급 신청 시 수입자가 구비해야 서류는 신청서, 수출수입자 간 계약서, KRS(National Court Register)등록 서류, 관세 적기납부증명서, VAT적기 납부증명서, Labor tax적기 납부증명서, 상세한 제품공정 설명서, 세관 보증서임

☐ 통관일로부터 6개월 이내에 수출되는 수입품의 경우에는 최초 징수된 관세의 100%가 환급되며 6개월에서 12개월 이내에 수출되는 경우에는 50%가 환급됨[52]

☐ 관세 과오납 환급의 경우 환급요건은 환급목적에 따라 HS Code 문제, FTA규정 오적용, 관세율 및 과세가격 오적용의 4가지로 구분함

---

[51] 관련 규정 KEP-205/BC/2003, SE-20/BC/2006
[52] 한국무역협회 홈페이지 http://www.kita.net

○ 과오납 환급은 ① 세관조사 취지 공문문서 발송 → ② 14일 이내 문제점 소명자료 요청 → ③ 세관의 답변 → ④ 30일 내 세관의 의사결정 → ⑤ 관세 환급 또는 지불의 과정으로 이루어짐

☐ HS Code 문제 시 제품 설명서나 전문가 의견서 또는 BTI 및 현지 업체 의견서를 제출하여야 하고, FTA규정 오적용의 경우 상업송장 원본을, 관세율 오적용은 관세율 정정 신청서를 제출해야 하며, 과세가격 오류는 수정된 상업송장 및 운송장을 제출해야 함

☐ 구입 부가세도 환급이 가능하며 환급은 최대 180일 내에 이루어짐
    ○ 부가세 환급은 ① 통관(부가세 납부) → ② 제조(15일) → ③ 출하(1주) → ④ 부가세 신고(차월 25일) → ⑤ 환급(신고 후 60일/수정 신고 시 이날부터 60일 기산)의 과정으로 이루어 짐
    ○ 기업이 인하된 부가세율 혹은 영세율로 과세되는 비즈니스 활동을 수행하거나, 구입 부가세가 고정자산 매입에 의한 것일 경우에는 환급 기한이 60일 혹은 25일까지 단축될 수 있음

Ⅳ. 통관 절차별 고려 사항

〈표 Ⅳ-1〉 폴란드 통관 절차별 유의사항

단 계	유 의 사 항
1. 수입 신고 전 준비 및 관세영역 도착	○ 공산품과 관련하여 폴란드에 물품 수입 시 EU회원국 전체에 적용되는 강제 기술규격 인증인 CE를 받아야 함 ○ 임시 개청제도를 운영하고 있으며 약식통관 절차 적용업체는 24시간 통관이 가능함 ○ 품목분류 사전심사 시 번역 혹은 폴란드 세관의 자의적인 해석에 따라 품목 분류 오류가 있었으므로 미리 유의해야 함 ○ 수입 전 EORI번호가 기입된 ENS를 반드시 제출해야 함 ○ 라벨 부착 대상 품목에는 폴란드어로 된 라벨을 부착해야 함 ○ 한·EU FTA 원산지 신고서는 수출자 자율발급이며 건당 수출금액이 6,000유로 초과 시에는 원산지 인증 수출자만 자율발급 가능 ○ 일부 품목은 덤핑방지 관세부과 등 규제가 있으므로 확인이 필요함
2. 수입 신고 및 세관 심사	○ 통관 단계별로 정형화되지 않은 서류 제출 요구가 있었으므로 수입 관련 서류를 미리 구비하는 것을 권고함 ○ 무관세 품목에 대해 원산지 증명 서류의 부족이나 기타 서류 부족 등의 이유로 지속적으로 관세를 요구하는 경우가 있음 ○ 검사는 세관의 선택에 따라 일반적으로 서류검사, 서류면제, 물품검사의 세 가지 방식으로 진행됨
3. 세금 납부 및 물품 반출	○ 관세유예제도(End Use Procedure)를 운영하고 있으며 제도의 적용 시마다 세관에서 계산서 요청이 있었으므로 미리 구비해야 함 ○ EU는 역내에서 수출입 화물과 관련한 승인을 하나의 회원국에서 받은 경우 기타 EU국가의 통관 시에도 적용받을 수 있는 Single Authority제도를 시행하고 있음
4. 수출 및 환급	○ 통관일로부터 6개월 이내에 수출되는 수입품의 경우에는 최초 징수된 관세의 100%가 환급되며 6개월에서 12개월 이내에 수출되는 경우에는 50%가 환급됨 ○ 관세 유예 적용 시에도 관세 환급과 마찬가지로 관세 적기 납부 증명서와 VAT 적기 납부 증명서를 제출해야함 ○ 원산지 인증 수출자가 아닌 업체의 경우 통관 후 2년 이내에 인증 수출자로 지정받아 원산지 신고서를 제출하면 FTA 협정관세가 사후 적용되어 환급 가능함

1. 수입 신고 전 준비

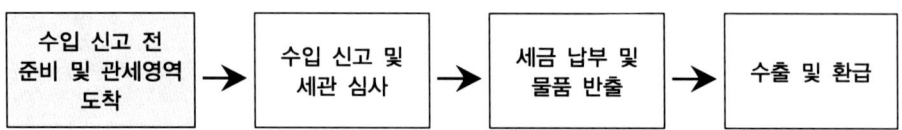

가. 통관 절차상 특이사항

☐ 운송인이나 대리인에 의해 세관에 제출된 물품은 개괄신고서에 의해 처리되며 물품의 세관 제출 시 단 1일 이내에 신고를 연기할 수 있음

☐ 운송인은 세관에 화물상세정보(물품명, HS code, 컨테이너 번호 등), 화물 운송인, 송하인, 수하인 등의 인적정보(AEO인증 여부 포함) 및 운송항로 등의 운항 정보를 제출해야 함

☐ 운송인은 EU에 화물이 도착하기 전에 적하목록의 전송을 완료해야 하며 기한 내 적하목록 미제출 1회 이상 혹은 적하목록 허위 제출 3회 이상의 경우 2012년 1월 1일부터 과태료 부과 대상이 됨

☐ 적하목록은 폴란드의 ICS(Import Control System)시스템을 통해서 전산으로 전송되며 ICS에 대한 자세한 안내 및 관련 서류는 관세청 홈페이지[53])에서 확인 가능함

☐ 폴란드로 수출하는 물품에 대해 FTA에 따른 특혜세율을 적용받기 위해서는 원산지 증명서(상업송장에 관세청으로부터 부여받은 원산지 인증 수출자 인증번호를 기재하는 것으로 대체)를 제시해야 함
  ○ 원산지 증명서에 명시된 물품 양과 통관 시 제출되는 물품 양의 편차는 10% 이상을 초과할 수 없음

---

53) http://www.mofnet.gov.pl/index.php?const=2&dzial=1962&wysw=84&sub=sub6

○ 원산지 증명서를 제시하지 않아도 수출은 가능하나 유럽의 수입자 입장에서는 기준 세율로 관세를 납부해야 하기에 상당한 불이익이 예상됨

□ 세관 제출 역외물품은 세관의 별도 인수 또는 사용허가를 득하여야 함
  ○ 개괄신고에 의한 통관 신고 후 세관의 인수 또는 사용허가를 받아야 하는 기간은 해상화물의 경우 신고서 제출 후 45일 이내이며 항공 및 기타화물은 개괄 신고서 제출 후 20일 이내임
    - 위의 기간 동안 수입 신고 전인 물품을 보관할 수 있으며 세관창고, 수입자 또는 화물 보관인의 창고 등에 일시적으로 물품을 장치할 수 있음
  ○ 일시적 보관물품은 세관이 정한 장소에 원형대로 보관되어야 하며, 특별 취급을 요하는 화물의 경우에는 운송인의 부담으로 별도 장소에 보관할 수 있음

□ 세관은 불법 반입 및 반출 화물이 발견될 시 혹은 통관 절차 처리기한이 경과한 물품에 대해 몰수, 매각을 포함한 제반 조치를 취할 수 있으며 이때 폐기 비용은 화주가 부담해야 함

나. 애로 사례

□ 세관이 오후 4시에 통관 업무를 종료하여 낮 12시 이후 통관 신청 시 당일 심사가 불가능하였으며 일선 세관에서는 임시 개청이 이루어지지 않은 경우가 있었음
  ○ 폴란드 세관은 현재 임시 개청제도를 운영하여 업무 시간 외 통관이 가능하며 약식 통관 절차 적용업체는 24시간 통관이 가능하다고 공식적으로 답변함

□ 원본서류 요구로 통관이 지연되는 사례가 종종 발생하므로 미리 준비해두어야 함
  ○ 회사 대표 부재 시 통관을 위해서 회사 대표의 자필 서명이 있는 통관 위임장을 요구한 경우가 있어 회사 대표의 귀국까지 통관이 지연된 경우가 있었음
  ○ 폴란드 세관은 한국 기업들이 통관 담당자에 대하여 1회용이 아닌 일정한 유효기간(6개월 혹은 1년)을 지닌 위임장을 발급할 것을 권장함[54]

□ 통관 관련 서류는 폴란드어로 번역을 해야 하며 이때 품명, 내용 등이 기술적이고 전문적이므로 번역에 많은 시간과 비용이 소요됨
　○ 폴란드어 품명을 기준으로 품목 분류를 하고 있기 때문에 번역에 따라 분류가 상이하게 되어 높은 관세가 부과되는 경우가 발생함

□ 폴란드로 수출하는 LCD 모듈에 대해 폴란드 관세당국이 관세율 0%인 LCD 모듈이 아닌 TV 기타 부분품으로 품목을 결정하여 5%의 관세율을 적용하였으나 한국 관세청의 노력으로 분쟁이 해결됨

□ 과거 특혜관세를 적용받기 위한 Euro 1 Movement Certificate[55])의 발급이 지연되는 경우가 발생한 적이 있었으므로 법적 신청일(150일) 이전에 신청할 것을 권장함

□ 일부 식품류의 경우 97년 1월 1일부터 유통기한, 보관 및 수송 방법에 대해 농업부 산하의 중앙표준검사소가 검사를 실시하고 있으며 식품 검역 증명서 및 기타 증명서 발급 시 장시간이 소요되어 통관이 지연되는 경우가 과거에 있었음

다. 업무상 유의점

□ 2011년 1월 1일부터 바뀐 EU의 수입 법에 따르면 도착 전 신고서(ENS)제출 및 수출 선적서류의 사본 제출 시 모든 서류에 EORI Number(Economic Operators Registration and Identification Number)를 기재해야만 함
　○ EORI번호는 각 EU국가별 개별 세관의 수출 및 수입자번호(Exporter/Importer code)를 EU에서 하나의 번호(code)로 통합한 것으로서 일종의 고객번호(Customer code)를 말함
　○ 한·EU 회원국 세관당국에 등록된 번호는 전 EU 회원국에서 공동으로 통용되므

---

54) 주 폴란드 대사관, 2008, 제2차 한·폴란드 관세청장회의 결과보고
55) Euro 1 Movement Certificate 는 EU 역외 국가로부터 원자재를 수입하여 EU 내에서 생산하고 EU 역외 국가로 수출하는 경우 일정 요건을 갖춘 품목에 한해 발급되는 일종의 EU 원산지 증명서로서 http://trade.ec.europa.eu/doclib/docs/2009/june/tradoc_143658.pdf에서 증명서 및 지침 다운 가능

로 다른 회원국 수출입 시 다시 번호를 받지 않아도 됨
- ENS 신고인이 AEO자격이 있어야 한다는 요구 사항은 없으나 제 3자가 선사를 대리하여 ENS 신고를 할 때에 제3자 자신의 EORI번호와 선사의 EORI번호를 함께 기재하여야 함

□ 화주(Shipper Consignee)의 EORI번호가 있으면 선적 의뢰서(S/R)에 포함시켜야 하며 지시 선하증권(To Order B/L)의 경우 통지처(Notify Party)의 EORI번호[56]가 필요함
- EORI번호가 없을 경우 화주의 Full name 및 상세주소가 요구되며 상세주소는 국가, 도시, 우편번호를 각각 독립된 데이터로 전송할 것을 요구함
- 웹사이트[57]에서 지원 번호, 지원 상태, 할당된 EORI번호를 확인할 수 있음
- EU 위원회의 웹사이트[58]에 방문하여 EORI번호가 유효한지 알 수 있으며 국가별로 이를 승인해주는 세관 또한 확인할 수 있음
- EORI의 데이터베이스는 24시간마다 늦은 시간에 업데이트되므로 적어도 하루가 지난 후에 검색이 가능함

□ 우리나라에서 폴란드로 물품 수출 전, 해당 품목이 덤핑방지관세 부과 등 규제 대상 품목인지 여부를 확인할 필요가 있음
- 덤핑방지관세 등이 부과되는 경우 수입자는 통관을 위해 예상치 못했던 높은 세금을 내야 하거나, 현지 수입상이 수입을 거절할 경우 물품이 한국으로 반송되는 경우도 발생할 수 있으므로 규제 사항을 사전에 확인해 두어야 함

□ 한국무역협회 통상·수입규제 홈페이지[59]에서는 세계 각국의 통상 현안을 비롯하여 국가별 반덤핑 및 상계관세 부과 정부 등 다양한 관련 정보를 제공하고 있음
- 한국무역협회 기본 홈페이지[60]에서는 하단 '사업별 사이트' 메뉴 중 '통상수입규

---

56) EORI 번호의 신청에 대한 가이드와 신청문서는 http://www.mofnet.gov.pl/index.php?const=2&dzial=2684&wysw=2&sub=sub7 에서 확인 가능
57) http://www.e-clo.pl/eori-subpage/index.jsp
58) http://ec.europa.eu/taxation_customs/dds2/eos/eos_home.jsp?Lang=en
59) http://antidumping.kita.net

제'로도 접속 가능함

○ 현재 폴란드가 반덤핑관세 등의 규제를 가하는 품목 확인을 위해서는 'KITA 통상·수입규제' 홈페이지 상단 메뉴 중 '수입규제 현황' → '주요국 제소 및 규제내역' → '유럽'에서 폴란드의 내용을 점검할 수 있음
  - 또한 '수입규제 현황' → '국가별 현황'에서는 필요 정보 지정 후 검색 기능을 통해 영문 품명과 정확한 HS코드 등 보다 세밀한 정보를 확인할 수 있음
○ 그 외에 WTO에서 반기별로 공개하는 국가별 규제 동향도 살펴볼 수 있는데, 이는 '통상·수입규제' 사이트 상단 메뉴 중 '각국 규제동향'에서 확인 가능함

□ 에너지 라벨링의 적용범위가 확대되고 있으며 특히 TV의 경우 2011년 11월부터 라벨링 부착이 의무화되었으므로 라벨링 규정을 사전에 확인해야 함

2. 수입 신고 및 세관 심사

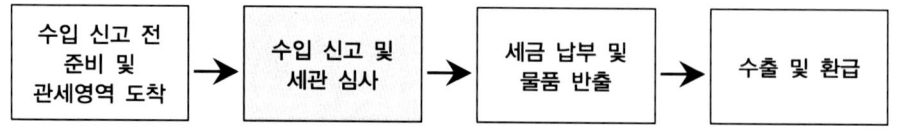

가. 통관 절차상 특이사항

□ 세관 검사는 일반적으로 운반트럭이 세관에 입고되면 세관에서 서류검사, 서류 검사 면제, 물품검사의 세 가지 검사 중 하나의 방법을 선택하여 검사함
  ○ 간소화 방식의 경우 세관 홈페이지에 수입신고 후 세관에서 세 가지 방식 중 하나를 정하여 검사하며 제품검사가 필요할 시 업체 창고에 세관 검사원이 대기하여 검사하게 됨

---

60) http://www.kita.net

□ 통관 신고 후 세관은 신고서에 최초 기재된 품목에 대하여 수정을 허가하나 물품 검사 통지를 한 경우에는 신고 무효가 검사 완료 시까지 불가하며 물품이 통관된 후 역시 신고 무효가 불가능함

□ 선하증권, 상업송장, 포장명세서 등은 필수 제출 서류이며, FTA 특혜 세율 적용 희망 시 원산지 신고서를, 세관의 요청 시에는 기타 요건 구비 증명자료를 제출해야 함

□ 검사의 결과는 부분검사의 결과를 전 신고품목에 확대 적용하며 이 결과에 불복할 경우 신고인은 계속 검사를 요구할 수 있음
  ○ 물품의 운송수단 또는 상표 등의 동일성 확인 수단은 세관에 의하거나 허가를 받아야만 제거 또는 폐기 가능함

□ 수입 통관에 필요한 서류를 모두 제대로 갖추었다는 전제하에 전산 처리만으로 통관이 가능한 경우는 수입신고 후 통관까지 약 0.2시간이 소요되며 세관에 서류 제출을 한 경우에는 2시간, 세관에서 물품 검사를 요구한 경우는 약 3~4시간이 소요됨

나. 애로 사례

□ 컨테이너 하역지와 상관없이 관할 세관이 지정하는 장소에서만 통관을 허가하여 물품비용이 증대한 경우가 있었으며 애로사항에 대해 폴란드 관세청에서는 업체신청 시 원하는 장소에서 통관할 수 있게 조치를 취하겠다고 답변함[61]

□ 품목별 및 통관 단계별 구비서류가 정형화되어 있지 않아 통관단계에서 시기를 달리하여 각종 서류제출을 요구한 경우가 있었음
  ○ 수입물품이 군사 용도나 흉기로 사용할 목적이 아니라는 증명서 등을 요구하여 통관이 지연된 사례가 있었음

---

[61] 주 폴란드 대사관, 2008, 「제2차 한·폴란드 관세청장회의 결과보고」

□ 무관세 품목에 대해 원산지 증명서류의 부족이나 기타 서류 부족 등의 이유로 지속적으로 관세를 요구하는 경우가 있으므로 증명서류를 완벽히 구비해야 함

다. 업무상 유의점

□ 수입신고 내용과 실제 품목, 또한 제출 서류상의 기재 사항(수입자와 수량, 중량, 품명, B/L 번호 및 컨테이너 번호 등)이 상호 정확히 일치하여 문제 발생의 소지가 없도록 작은 부분까지 철저를 기하도록 함
  ○ 신고인은 물품검사에 따른 제반 협조 제공 및 비용 부담에 대한 책임을 지며 검사 및 견본 검사 시 입회권을 가짐
  ○ 서류 검사 시 신고서 및 첨부서류의 기재사항 확인을 위해 추가서류 제출을 요구하는 경우가 있으므로 관련 서류를 미리 구비하는 것을 권고함
  ○ 화물 검사 시, 서류 및 신고한 내용과 실제 화물이 일치하지 않는 경우 밀수 행위로 간주될 수 있으므로, 서류와 물품 일치에 만전을 기해야 함

3. 세금 납부 및 물품 반출

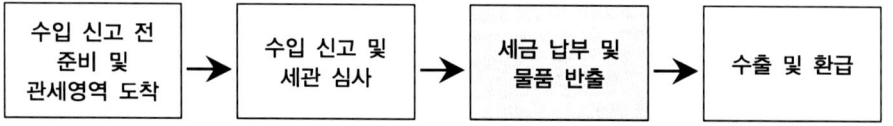

가. 통관 절차상 특이사항

□ 통관신고 접수일 이후 통관 이전까지 수입화물에 부과된 관세가 인하된 경우에 신고인은 보다 저율의 관세 적용을 요구할 수 있으나, 신고인의 귀책사유로 통관이 지연된 경우에는 적용을 배제함

□ EU는 역내에서 수출입 화물과 관련한 승인을 하나의 회원국에서 받은 경우 기타 EU 국가의 통관 시에도 적용받을 수 있는 Single Authority 제도를 시행하고 있음[62]
  ○ Single Authority 신청서는 통관이 일어나는 장소의 세관장[63]에게 제출되어야 하며 해당 신청 조건과, 기준국 준수 여부를 따랐을 경우 세관당국은 요청을 승인할 수 있음
  ○ 승인 기간은 세관당국이 승인에 필요한 모든 정보를 수신하는 날로부터 시작되며 세관당국은 신청자에게 시작 날짜를 통지해야 할 의무가 있음[64]

□ 역내 가공절차하의 관세 환급, 하자 및 위약 물품에 대한 관세 환급 시, 또한 통관 신고의 하자 등을 이유로 한 통관 무효 시 자유유통을 위해 통관된 물품은 역내물품으로서의 관세 지위를 상실함

나. 애로 사례

□ 브로츠와프 세관에서 Single Authority를 승인해주지 않아 오스트리아 및 독일을 통해 긴급 자재를 폴란드로 반입하며 통관국가의 세관에 관세를 납부하게 된 경우가 있었음

□ 폴란드에서는 관세유예제도(End Use Procedure)[65]를 운영하고 있으나 제도의 적용 승인을 받더라도 실제 적용 시마다 세관에서 복잡한 계산서 제출 요청이 있어 환급이 지연됨
  ○ 관세유예제도에 Single Authority 제도가 적용되므로 폴란드에서 관세유예 승인을 받았다면 기디 EU 국가 통관 때에도 관세유예 혜택을 받을 수 있으며 이때 Single

---

[62] 주 폴란드 대사관, 2008, 「제2차 한·폴란드 관세청장회의 결과보고」
[63] 폴란드 내 신청 가능 세관 목록은 http://ec.europa.eu/taxation_customs/resources/documents/customs/procedural_aspects/general/centralised_clearance/contact_points_pl_en.pdf에서 다운
[64] Single Authority에 관한 자세한 규정과 지침은 http://ec.europa.eu/taxation_customs/customs/procedural_aspects/general/centralised_clearance/index_en.htm에서 확인 가능함
[65] 관세유예제도는 EU에서 생산되지 않는 품목에 한하여 정해진 용도로 사용되어 EU 내에서만 유통된다는 조건하에 일정기간 낮은 세율 또는 영세율을 적용받는 제도임

Authority 신청서는 승인받고자 하는 세관[66]에 제출하면 됨
- 동 제도를 적용하여 담보 설정 후 무관세로 통관하더라도 담보 회복을 위해 제출해야 하는 서류가 복잡하여 담보가 계속 증액되는 사례가 발생함

다. 업무상 유의점

□ 화물이 신고된 회원국에서 물품이 판매될 시 관세와 부가가치세, 개인소비세 등 간접세를 해당국에 지불해야 하지만 다른 회원국으로 통과(Transit)될 경우 납세행위는 유보됨

□ 상이한 품목분류에 의해 물품이 반출될 경우 세관은 신고인의 동의를 얻어 품목 중 가장 높은 관세 수준을 기초로 전 품목에 대한 관세를 부과할 수 있음

4. 수출 및 환급

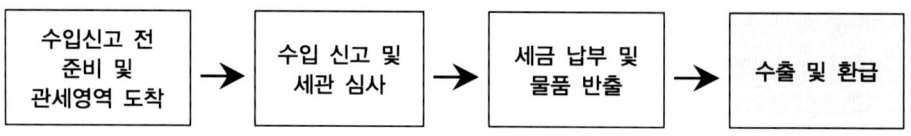

가. 통관 절차상 특이사항

□ 세관은 가공생산품의 수출신고서 접수 시 환급허가를 부여하며, 통관 신고 시에 환급 대상 품목임을 명시한 후 환급허가명세서 및 SAD를 함께 첨부 후 제출하여 신청해야 함

---

[66] 관세유예와 관련한 Single Authority 제도의 적용 지침은 http://ec.europa.eu/taxation_customs/customs/procedural_aspects/general/single_authorisation/index_en.htm에서 확인

□ 관세 유예제도 적용 시 구비서류는 관세 환급을 위한 구비서류 목록[67]과 동일하며 이때 관세 적기납부 증명서와 VAT 적기납부 증명서는 약속이행서의 개념으로써 관세와 VAT를 납부하겠다는 전제 하에 세관에서 발행해 주는 것임

□ 세관은 독자적 혹은 신고인의 요구로 통관 후 관련업무 및 신고서, 첨부서류 등을 사후 심사할 수 있음
  ○ 심사는 신고인 또는 관계인의 사무실에서 행하며, 통관 물품의 제조과정이 계속되는 경우에는 사후 심사를 계속 할 수 있음

나. 애로 사례

□ 관세 환급 기간이 예상 기간(약 6개월)보다 긴 편이며 실제 환급에 있어서는 적어도 6개월에서 1년 이상이 소요됨

□ 수출용 원부자재에 대한 부가세(VAT) 환급 기간이 긴 편이며 구비해야 하는 서류도 복잡함
  ○ 환급기한인 60일이 준수되지 않고 실제 환급에 90일이 걸리는 경우가 빈번함
  ○ 수정신고가 자주 발생하며 이에 따라 환급이 지연되는 경우가 빈번함

□ 폴란드는 부가가치세 납부유예제도를 이행하지 않기 때문에 폴란드에 있는 수입업체가 독일이나 네덜란드 등 납부유예제도를(납부유예기간 약 30일) 이행하는 국가를 통해 통관하며 이 경우 환급까지 약 1년 이상이 소요됨

□ DDP(Delivered and Duty Paid)조건[68]으로 수출할 시 폴란드 세관이 수입국에 납부할 관세, 부가세를 제출할 것을 요구함

---

[67] 신청서, 수출수입자 간 계약서, KRS(National Court Register) 등록 서류, 관세 적기 납부증명서, VAT 적기 납부 증명서, Labor tax 적기납부 증명서, 상세한 제품공정 설명서, 세관 보증서
[68] DDP는 지정 목적지 관세지급인도 조건이란 표현으로 수출자가 물건을 수입자에게 인도할 때까지 모든 비용(수출 비용, 운임, 수입국 관세 및 조세부과금)을 부담하는 거래 조건을 말함

○ 이로 인해 정확한 세액산정 및 수출 및 수입 업체 간 사후 정산에 있어 애로사항이 발생하고 있으므로 폴란드에서 물품을 제조하여 수출하는 업체의 경우 미리 서류를 구비해야함

다. 업무상 유의점

☐ 관세 및 부가세 환급이 정해진 기간보다 지연되므로 사업 및 자금 계획에 있어 이를 감안하는 것이 필요함

☐ 역내 가공[69]의 경우 수입 원재료에 대해 제세의 납부유예 및 환급이 가능하며 역외 가공[70]의 경우 재수입된 역외 가공 생산품은 수입관세의 전부 또는 일부가 면제됨

☐ 원산지 인증 수출자가 아닌 업체의 경우 통관 후 2년 내에 인증 수출자로 지정받아 원산지 신고서를 제출하면 FTA 협정관세가 사후 적용되어 환급이 가능함

☐ 폴란드는 부가가치세 환급을 법으로 규정하고 있으나 실제 환급을 신청할 경우 현지 확인 조사 후에 환급금을 지급함

☐ 고세율의 원재료로 저세율의 제품을 역내에서 가공하여 자유 유통시킬 경우 특별한 세관 통제를 받으며 통제를 받는 해당 원재료 등은 EU 집행위에서 별도로 규정하기 때문에 미리 확인해야 함
　○ 예를 들어 PVC재료는 8.3%의 관세율인 반면, film screen의 경우에는 2.7%의 관세율이 부과됨

---

[69] 역내 가공: 역외로부터 수입한 물품을 원료로 EU 내에서 제조한 물품을 역외로 재수출하는 것
[70] 역외 가공: 역내 물품을 EU 영역으로부터 일시적으로 반출하여 역외에서 제조, 가공한 후 수입하는 것

참고문헌

외교통상부, 『2011 외국의 통상환경』, 2011. 2

USTR, 「National Trade Estimate Report on Foreign Trade Barriers」, 2012. 3
The World Bank Group, 「Doing Business 2012」, 2012

관세무역개발원 www.custra.com
대한민국 관세청, www.customs.go.kr
대한무역투자진흥공사 폴란드 KBC, www.kotra.or.kr
대한상공회의소, www.korcham.net
대한상공회의소 국제통상정보서비스, www.global.korcham.net
미국 무역 대표부, www.ustr.gov
세계은행, www.doingbusiness.org
세계무역기구, www.wto.org
산업연구원 해외산업정보 kiet.go.kr/servlet/isearch
외교통상부, www.mofat.go.kr
전 세계 FTA 현황, www.bilaterals.org
지식경제부 기술 표준원, www.tbt.kr
주한 폴란드 대사관 무역 투자 진흥부 www seoul.trade.gov.pl/ko/o_nas
폴란드 관세청 www.mofnet.gov.pl/?const=2&lang=en
폴란드 상공회의소 www.chamberofcommerce.pl/export-poland/
폴란드 재무부 www.mf.gov.pl/index.php?const=1
한국무역협회, www.kita.net
한국무역협회 블로그 blog.naver.com/kitablog

해외진출 정보시스템, www.ois.go.kr

Trade Related Rule Book, protraf.net/rulebook

부록 Ⅰ. 비즈니스 팁

□ 폴란드 관공서는 대부분 오전 8시에 업무를 시작하고 오후 4시에 업무를 종료함
  ○ 폴란드인들은 가족과 함께하는 문화를 다소 중요시하기 때문에 근무시간을 정확히 지키는 편이며 회식은 드문 편임

□ 폴란드의 수입품 유통 구조는 수입상 → 디스트리뷰터 → 도매상 → 소매상과 같은 전형적인 형태가 아니며 후르토브니아(Hurtownia, 자체 창고를 보유한 도매상)를 겸하는 수입상이 수입부터 도매까지 겸하는 경우가 대부분임
  ○ 이들 수입상은 원·부자재를 생산 공장에 직접 공급하며 수입한 상품을 러시아와 주변 동구권에 재수출하기도 함

□ 국내 시장의 불안정, 대량 주문 생산에 필요한 자금력 부족, 소량 다품종 구매 등의 요인으로 스톡 수입 방식이 성행함
  ○ 디자인, 패션 등 소비 행태가 자주 바뀌는 대부분의 소비재가 이에 해당됨

□ 수입관세 및 부가세 절감을 위한 이면계약과 거래 대금의 과소신고(Under-Value Invoice) 요구가 많으며 이는 현지 마케팅 수행의 애로요인으로 작용하고 있음

□ 폴란드 바이어들은 일반적으로 신용장(L/C) 거래를 선호하지 않으며 대부분 송금(T/T) 혹은 외상거래(D/P, D/A)를 선호함
  ○ 신용장 개설 시 거래 은행의 현금 담보 요구(110%), 수입상의 자금 부족 등의 요인과 함께 외상거래를 선호하는 동구권의 일반적인 상관습에 따른 것임
  ○ 바이어가 제품을 마음에 들어 할 경우 신용장 거래를 수용하기도 하나 거래가 누적되었을 시 현금 분할 지급이나 외상거래와 같은 방식을 요구하는 경우가 많음

○ 초기 거래의 경우 대금의 10~30%를 선 지급하고 나머지는 제품이 폴란드 항구 도착 직전 또는 직후에 지급하는 방법(해상운송의 경우) 혹은 나머지를 선적 전에 지급하는 방법(항공운송이 경우)을 많이 사용하며 이때 잔금을 입금한 후 B/L을 보내게 됨
○ D/P나 D/A 거래의 경우 대금의 10~30%를 선금으로 받고 나머지를 D/A 60일의 조건으로 하는 방식도 가능함

□ 인사 시 호칭은 남자의 경우 폴란드어로 Pan(판), 여성은 Pani(결혼 여부에 관계없음)라고 하며 미국식의 Mr.나 Ms.도 일반적으로 사용됨
○ 여성과 인사할 때 남성은 목례로 인사하며 악수는 여성이 청할 때에만 함

□ 폴란드에서는 처음 만난 사람에게(바이어 포함) 선물을 주는 전통이 없기 때문에 초면의 바이어에게 과한 선물을 주면 당황할 수 있음
○ 회사 로고가 표시된 판촉물(펜, 노트, 작은 달력 등) 정도의 선물이 무난함

□ 바이어와 약속을 잡기 위해서는 최소 1주 전에 연락을 해두어야 하고 대체적으로 폴란드 사람들은 느긋한 편이므로 회신을 재촉한다면 좋지 않은 인상을 주게 됨

□ 폴란드 바이어들은 제품이 유망할 경우 독점 에이전트를 요구하는 경향이 있으나 거래 초기 서로 모르는 단계에서는 주의를 기울여야 함

□ 폴란드 사람들은 따로 가리는 음식이 없기 때문에 특별히 피할 음식도 없음
○ 최근 폴란드인 중 초밥을 즐기는 사람들이 늘어나고 있고 한식도 매운 음식 외에는 잘 먹는 편이므로 한국 식당에서 식사를 해도 무방함
○ 식사 시 마시는 술로는 맥주나 보드카가 대표적임
○ 폴란드인은 대체적으로 정찬 시 시간을 두고 느긋하게 즐기는 편임

□ 폴란드가 배출한 세계적 인물들에 대해 이야기하면 화기애애한 분위기를 조성할 수

있음
- ○ 폴란드의 위인으로 코페르니쿠스(지동설), 쇼팽, 퀴리부인, 교황 요한 바오로 2세 등이 있으며 한국에 알려진 자유 노조 지도자 바웬사에 관해서는 평가가 엇갈리기 때문에 언급을 피하는 것이 좋음

☐ 폴란드에서 대화하며 눈길을 피하는 것은 거짓말을 하거나 감추고 있다는 의미로 받아들여짐

☐ 유럽사회는 일반적으로 사생활을 중시하므로 개인적인 질문은 삼가는 것이 좋음
- ○ 프라이버시와 관련된 질문으로는 남자(여자)친구, 남편(부인) 관련사항, 자녀 관련 사항, 나이 관련 사항, 월급 등 금전 관련 사항, 종교, 정치 관련 사항 등이 있음
- ○ 이와 더불어 사람의 몸에 손을 대는 것을 싫어하며 악수할 때 손을 너무 오래 잡고 있는 것도 예의가 아님

☐ 간단한 폴란드어를 구사할 수 있으면 친밀감을 높이는 데 도움이 됨
- ○ 안녕하세요: 지엔 도브리(Dzien Dobry)
- ○ 안녕히 계세요: 슬라맛 띵갈(Selamat tinggal)
- ○ 안녕히 가십시오: 슬라맛 잘란(Selamat jalan)
- ○ 또 만나요: 도 비제니아(Do widzenia)
- ○ 감사합니다: 지엔쿠예(Dziekuje)
- ○ 천만에요: 끔발리(Kembali)
- ○ 죄송합니다: 마앞(Maaf)
- ○ 실례합니다: 뻬르미씨(Permisi)

부록 Ⅱ. 주요 유관 기관 정보

■ 주 폴란드 대한민국 대사관

웹페이지	pol.mofat.go.kr
주소	ul. Szwolezerow 6 00-464 Warssaw, Poland
이메일	koremb_waw@mofat.go.kr
전화번호	(48-22) 559-2900(대표)
팩스번호	(48-22) 559-2905

■ 문화원

웹페이지	pl.korean-culture.org
주소	ul. Kruczkowskiego 8 00-380 Warsaw, Poland
전화번호	(48-22) 525-0930
팩스번호	(48-22) 525-0939
이메일	kulturakoreanska@gmail.com

■ KOTRA 바르샤바 무역관(KBC)

웹페이지	www.kotra.or.kr - 해외무역관 - 바르샤바 무역관
주소	21th Fl. Warsaw Financial Center ul. Emilii Plater 53, 00-113 Warszawa, Poland
전화번호	(48-22) 520-6230
팩스번호	(48-22) 520-6231
이메일	biuro@kotra.pl

■ 폴란드 한인회

웹페이지	http://koreanpl.org/xe/
주소	사무실 없음
전화번호	(48) 602-662-033 (한인회 회장 핸드폰)
이메일	janusz@naver.com(한인회 회장)

■ 주한 폴란드 대사관 무역투자진흥부

웹페이지	http://www.seoul.trade.gov.pl/ko
주소	서울시 용산구 한남동 604 동경빌딩 4층 140-210
전화번호	(82-2) 3785-2471
팩스번호	(82-2) 797-0853
이메일	seoul@trade.gov.pl

■ 폴란드 재무부(Ministry of Finance)

웹페이지	http://www.mofnet.gov.pl/index.php?const=1
주소	ul. Świętokrzyska 1200-916 Warszawa,
전화번호	(48-22) 694-5555
팩스번호	(48-22) 694-4177 (Press Office)
이메일	kancelaria@mf.gov.pl

■ 폴란드 관세청(Customs Service)

웹페이지	http://www.mofnet.gov.pl/index.php?const=2
주소	ul. Hercena 1150-950 Wrocł aw Polska/Poland(국제협력과)
전화번호	(48-33) 857-6251
팩스번호	(48-71) 370-5497
이메일	info.sluzbacelna@kat.mofnet.gov.pl

■ 폴란드 해외투자 진흥청(Foreign Investment Agency)

웹페이지	http://www.paiz.gov.pl/en?lang_id=12
주소	ul. Bagatela 12; 00-585 Warsaw;
팩스번호	(48-22) 334-9889 (전화번호 없음)
이메일	invest@paiz.gov.pl

■ 폴란드 외무부(Ministry of Foreign Affairs)

웹페이지	http://www.msz.gov.pl/Strona,glowna,1.html
주소	Szucha 23, 00-580 Warsaw
전화번호	(48-22) 523-8188 (아시아지역)
팩스번호	(48-22) 523-9599 (아시아지역)
이메일	DAP.Sekretariat@msz.gov.pl (아시아지역)

■ 폴란드 통계청

웹페이지	http://www.stat.gov.pl/gus/index_ENG_HTML.htm
주소	00-925 Warsaw, Al. Niepodleg ł ości 208
전화번호	(48-22) 608-3000
팩스번호	(48-22) 608-3869 (정보센터)
이메일	obslugaprasowa@stat.gov.pl(홍보센터)

■ 폴란드 상공회의소

웹페이지	http://en.kig.pl/
주소	00-074 Warsaw, Trebacka 4 Street
전화번호	(48-22) 630-9600
팩스번호	(48-22) 827-4673
이메일	(48-22) 827-4673

부록 Ⅲ. EU Customs Code(EU 관세법)

COUNCIL REGULATION (EEC) No 2913/92 of 12 October 1992
establishing the Community Customs Code
(OJ L 302, 19.10.1992, p. 1)

Amended by: Official Journal
- ► M1 Regulation (EC) No 82/97 of the European Parliament and of the Council of 19 December 1996 L 17 1 21.1.1997
- ► M2 Regulation (EC) No 955/1999 of the European Parliament and of the Council of 13 April 1999 L 119 1 7.5.1999
- ► M3 Regulation (EC) No 2700/2000 of the European Parliament and of the Council of 16 November 2000 L 311 17 12.12.2000
- ► M4 Regulation (EC) No 648/2005 of the European Parliament and of the Council of 13 April 2005 L 117 13 4.5.2005
- ► M5 Council Regulation (EC) No 1791/2006 of 20 November 2006 L 363 1 20.12.2006

Amended by:
- ► A1 Act of Accession of Austria, Sweden and Finland C 241 21 29.8.1994 (adapted by Council Decision 95/1/EC, Euratom, ECSC) L 1 1 1.1.1995
- ► A2 Act concerning the conditions of accession of the Czech Republic, the Republic of Estonia, the Republic of Cyprus, the Republic of Latvia, the Republic of Lithuania, the Republic of Hungary, the Republic of Malta, the Republic of Poland, the Republic of Slovenia and the Slovak Republic and the adjustments to the Treaties on which the European Union is foundedL 236 33 23.9.2003

Corrected by:
- ► C1 Corrigendum, OJ L 152, 11.6.1997, p. 34 (2913/92)

► C2 Corrigendum, OJ L 179, 8.7.1997, p. 11 (82/97)

NB: This consolidated version contains references to the European unit of account and/or the ecu, which from 1 January 1999 should be understood as references to the euro — Council Regulation (EEC) No 3308/80 (OJ L 345, 20.12.1980, p. 1) andCouncil Regulation (EC) No 1103/97 (OJ L 162, 19.6.1997, p. 1).

COUNCIL REGULATION (EEC) No 2913/92of 12 October 1992 establishing the Community Customs Code

THE COUNCIL OF THE EUROPEAN COMMUNITIES,

Having regard to the Treaty establishing the European Economic Community, and in particular Articles 28, 100a and 113 thereof,

Having regard to the proposal from the Commission (1)[71],

In cooperation with the European Parliament (2),[72]

Having regard to the opinion of the Economic and Social Committee (3)[73],

Whereas the Community is based upon a customs union; whereas it is advisable, in the interests both of Community traders and the customs authorities, to assemble in a code the provisions of customs legislation that are at present contained in a large number of Community regulations and directives; whereas this task is of fundamental importance from the standpoint of the internal market;

Whereas such a Community Customs Code (hereinafter called 'the Code') must incorporate current customs legislation; whereas it is, nevertheless, advisable to amend that legislation in order to make it more consistent, to simplify it and to remedy certain omissions that still exist with a view to adopting complete Community legislation in this area;

---

71) OJ No C 128, 23.5.1990, p. 1.

72) OJ No C 72, 18.3.1991, p. 176 and Decision of 16 September 1992 (not yet published in the Official Journal).

73) OJ No C 60, 8.3.1991, p. 5.

Whereas, based on the concept of an internal market, the Code must contain the general rules and procedures which ensure the implementation of the tariff and other measures introduced at Community level in connection with trade in goods between the Community and third countries; whereas it must cover, among other things, the implementation of common agricultural and commercial policy measures taking into account the requirements of these common policies;

Whereas it would appear advisable to specify that this Code is applicable without prejudice to specific provisions laid down in other fields; whereas such specific rules may exist or be introduced in the context, inter alia, of legislation relating to agriculture, statistics, commercial policy or own resources;

Whereas, in order to secure a balance between the needs of the customs authorities in regard to ensuring the correct application of customs legislation, on the one hand, and the right of traders to be treated fairly, on the other, the said authorities must be granted, inter alia, extensive powers of control and the said traders a right of appeal; whereas the implementation of a customs appeals system will require the United Kingdom to introduce new administrative procedures which cannot be effected before 1 January 1995;

Whereas in view of the paramount importance of external trade for the Community, customs formalities and controls should be abolished or at least kept to a minimum;

Whereas it is important to guarantee the uniform application of this Code and to provide, to that end, for a Community procedure which enables the procedures for its implementation to be adopted within a suitable time; whereas a Customs Code Committee should be set up in

order to ensure close and effective cooperation between the Member States and the Commission in this field;

Whereas in adopting the measures required to implement this Code, the utmost care must be taken to prevent any fraud or irregularity liable to affect adversely the General Budget of the European Communities,

HAS ADOPTED THIS REGULATION:

TITLE I
GENERAL PROVISIONS

CHAPTER 1
SCOPE AND BASIC DEFINITIONS

Article 1

Customs rules shall consist of this Code and the provisions adopted at Community level or nationally to implement them. The Code shall apply, without prejudice to special rules laid down in other fields

- to trade between the Community and third countries,
- to goods covered by the Treaty establishing the European Coal and Steel Community, the Treaty establishing the European Economic Community or the Treaty establishing the European Atomic Energy Community.

Article 2

1. Save as otherwise provided, either under international conventions or customary practices of a limited geographic and economic scope or under autonomous Community measures, Community customs rules shall apply uniformly throughout the customs territory of the Community.

2. Certain provisions of customs rules may also apply outside the customs territory of the Community within the framework of either rules governing specific fields or international conventions.

Article 3

▼A1

1. The customs territory of the Community shall comprise:
   - the territory of the Kingdom of Belgium,
   - the territory of the Kingdom of Denmark, except the Faroe Islandsand Greenland,
   - the territory of the Federal Republic of Germany, except the Islandof Heligoland and the erritory of Büsingen (Treaty of 23 November 1964 between the Federal Republic of

Germany and the Swiss Confederation),
- the territory of the Hellenic Republic,
- the territory of the Kingdom of Spain, except Ceuta and Melilla,

▼M1
- the territory of the French Republic, except the overseas territories and Saint-Pierre and Miquelon and Mayotte

▼A1
- the territory of Ireland,
- the territory of the Italian Republic, except the municipalities of Livigno and Campione d'Italia and the national waters of Lake

▼B
Lugano which are between the bank and the political frontier of the area between Ponte Tresa and Porto Ceresio,
- the territory of the Grand Duchy of Luxembourg,
- the territory of the Kingdom of the Netherlands in Europe,
- the territory of the Republic of Austria,
- the territory of the Portuguese Republic,

▼M1
- the territory of the Republic of Finland,

▼A1
- the territory of the Kingdom of Sweden,
- the territory of the United Kingdom of Great Britain and Northern Ireland and of the Channel Islands and the Isle of Man,

▼A2
- the territory of the Czech Republic,
- the territory of the Republic of Estonia,
- the territory of the Republic of Cyprus,
- the territory of the Republic of Latvia,
- the territory of the Republic of Lithuania,
- the territory of the Republic of Hungary,
- the territory of the Republic of Malta,

- the territory of the Republic of Poland,
- the territory of the Republic of Slovenia,
- the territory of the Slovak Republic,

▼M5

- the territory of the Republic of Bulgaria,
- the territory of Romania.

▼A2

2. The following territories situated outside the territory of the Member States shall, taking the conventions and treaties applicable to them into account, be considered to be part of the customs territory of the Community:

(a) FRANCE

The territory of the principality of Monaco as defined in the Customs Convention signed in Paris on 18 May 1963 (Official Journal of the French Republic of 27 September 1963, p. 8679)

(b) CYPRUS

The territory of the United Kingdom Sovereign Base Areas of Akrotiri and Dhekelia as defined in the Treaty concerning the Establishment of the Republic of Cyprus, signed in Nicosia on 16 August 1960 (United Kingdom Treaty Series No 4 (1961) Cmnd. 1252).

▼B

3. The customs territory of the Community shall include the territorial waters, the inland maritime waters and the airspace of the Member States, and the territories referred to in paragraph 2, except for the territorial waters, the inland maritime waters and the airspace of those territories which are not part of the customs territory of the Community pursuant to paragraph 1.

Article 4

For the purposes of this Code, the following definitions shall apply:

▼A1

(1) 'Person' means:
 - a natural person,
 - a legal person,

- where the possibility is provided for under the rules in force, an association of persons recognized as having the capacity to perform legal acts but lacking the legal status of a legal person.
(2) 'Persons established in the Community' means:
  - in the case of a natural person, any person who is normally resident there,
  - in the case of a legal person or an association of persons, any person that has in the Community its registered office, central headquarters or a permanent business establishment.
(3) 'Customs authorities' means the authorities responsible inter alia for applying customs rules.
(4) 'Customs office' means any office at which all or some of the formalities laid down by customs rules may be completed.

▼M4

(4a) 'Customs office of entry' means the customs office designated by the customs authorities in accordance with the customs rules to which goods brought into the customs territory of the Community must be conveyed without delay and at which they will be subject to appropriate risk-based entry controls.

(4b) 'Customs office of import' means the customs office designated by the customs authorities in accordance with the customs rules wherethe formalities for assigning goods brought into the customs territory of the Community to a customs-approved treatment or use, including appropriate risk-based controls, are to be carried out.

(4c) 'Customs office of export' means the customs office designated bythe customs authorities in accordance with the customs rules where the formalities for assigning goods leaving the customs territory of the Community to a customs-approved treatment or use, including appropriate risk-based controls, are to be completed.

(4d) 'Customs office of exit' means the customs office designated by he customs authorities in accordance with the customs rules to which goods must be presented before they leave the customs territory of the Community and at which they will be subject to customs controls relating to the completion of exit formalities, and appropriate risk-based controls.

▼B

(5) 'Decision' means any official act by the customs authoritiespertaining to customs rules giving a ruling on a particular case, such act having legal effects on one or more specific or identifiable persons; ►M1 this term covers, inter alia, binding information within the meaning of Article 12. ◄

(6) 'Customs status' means the status of goods as Community or non- Community goods.

(7) 'Community goods' means goods:

▼M1

- wholly obtained in the customs territory of the Community under the conditions referred to in Article 23 and not incorporating goods imported from countries or territories not forming part of the customs territory of the Community. Goods obtained from goods placed under a suspensive arrangement shall not be deemed to have Community status in cases of special economic importance determined in accordance with the committee procedure,

▼B

- imported from countries or territories not forming part of the customs territory of the Community which have been released for free circulation,
- obtained or produced in the customs territory of the Community, either from goods referred to in the second indent alone or from goods referred to in first and second indents.

(8) 'Non-Community goods' means goods other than those referred to in subparagraph 7. Without prejudice to Articles 163 and 164, Community goods shall lose their status as such when they are actually removed from the customs territory of the Community.

(9) 'Customs debt' means the obligation on a person to pay the amount of the import duties (customs debt on importation) or export duties (customs debt on exportation) which apply to specific goods under the Community provisions in force.

(10) 'Import duties' means:

- customs duties and charges having an effect equivalent to customs duties payable on the importation of goods,
- ►M1 _____ ◄ import charges introduced under the common agricultural policy or under the specific arrangements applicable to certain goods resulting from the processing of agricultural products.

(11) 'Export duties' means:
   - customs duties and charges having an effect equivalent to customs duties payable on the exportation of goods,
   - ►M1 _____ ◄ export charges introduced under the common agricultural policy or under the specific arrangements applicable to certain goods resulting from the processing of agricultural products.
(12) 'Debtor' means any person liable for payment of a customs debt.
(13) 'Supervision by the customs authorities' means action taken in general by those authorities with a view to ensuring that customs rules and, where appropriate, other provisions applicable to goods subject to customs supervision are observed.
▼M4
(14) 'Customs controls' means specific acts performed by the customs authorities in order to ensure the correct application of customs rules and other legislation governing the entry, exit, transit, transfer and end-use of goods moved between the customs territory of the Community and third countries and the presence of goods that do not have Community status; such acts may include examining goods, verifying declaration data and the existence and authenticity of electronic or written documents, examining the accounts of undertakings and other records, inspecting means of transport, inspecting luggage and other goods carried by or on persons and carrying out official inquiries and other similar acts.
▼B
(15) 'Customs-approved treatment or use of goods' means:
   (a) the placing of goods under a customs procedure;
   (b) their entry into a free zone or free warehouse;
   (c) their re-exportation from the customs territory of the Community;
   (d) their destruction;
   (e) their abandonment to the Exchequer.
▼B
(16) 'Customs procedure' means:
   (a) release for free circulation;

(b) transit;

(c) customs warehousing;

(d) inward processing;

(e) processing under customs control;

(f) temporary admission;

(g) outward processing;

(h) exportation.

(17) 'Customs declaration' means the act whereby a person indicates in the prescribed form and manner a wish to place goods under a given customs procedure.

(18) 'Declarant' means the person making the customs declaration in his own name or the person in whose name a customs declaration is made.

(19) 'Presentation of goods to customs' means the notification to the customs authorities, in the manner laid down, of the arrival of goods at the customs office or at any other place designated or approved by the customs authorities.

(20) 'Release of goods' means the act whereby the customs authorities make goods available for the purposes stipulated by the customs procedure under which they are placed.

(21) 'Holder of the procedure' means the person on whose behalf the customs declaration was made or the person to whom the rights and obligations of the abovementioned person in respect of a customs procedure have been transferred.

(22) 'Holder of the authorization' means the person to whom an authorization has been granted.

(23) 'Provisions in force' means Community or national provisions.

▼M3

(24) Committee procedure means either the procedure referred to in Articles 247 and 247a, or in Articles 248 and 248a.

▼M4

(25) 'Risk' means the likelihood of an event occurring, in connection with the entry, exit, transit, transfer and end-use of goods moved between the customs territory of the Community and third countries and the presence of goods that do not have Community status, which

- prevents the correct application of Community or national measures, or
- compromises the financial interests of the Community and its Member States, or
- poses a threat to the Community's security and safety, to public health, to the environment or to consumers.

(26) 'Risk management' means the systematic identification of risk and implementation of all measures necessary for limiting exposure to risk. This includes activities such as collecting data and information, analysing and assessing risk, prescribing and taking action and regular monitoring and review of the process and its outcomes, based on international, Community and national sources and strategies.

▼B

CHAPTER 2
SUNDRY GENERAL PROVISIONS RELATING IN PARTICULAR TO THE RIGHTS AND OBLIGATIONS OF PERSONS WITH REGARD TO CUSTOMS RULES

Section 1
Right of representation

Article 5

1. Under the conditions set out in Article 64 (2) and subject to the provisions adopted within the framework of Article 243 (2) (b), any person may appoint a representative in his dealings with the customs authorities to perform the acts and formalities laid down by customs rules.

2. Such representation may be:
   - direct, in which case the representative shall act in the name of and on behalf of another person, or
   - indirect, in which case the representatives shall act in his own name but on behalf of another person. A Member State may restrict the right to make customs declarations:
   - by direct representation, or
   - by indirect representation, so that the representative must be a customs agent carrying on his business in that country's territory.

3. Save in the cases referred to in Article 64 (2) (b) and (3), a representative must be established within the Community.

4. A representative must state that he is acting on behalf of the person represented, specify whether the representation is direct or indirect and be empowered to act as a representative. A person who fails to state that he is acting in the name of or on behalf of another person or who states that he is acting in the name of or on behalf of another person without being empowered to do so shall be deemed to be acting in his own name and on his own behalf.

5. The customs authorities may require any person stating that he is acting in the name of or on behalf of another person to produce evidence of his powers to act as a representative.

▼M4

Section 1A
Authorised economic operators

Article 5a

1. Customs authorities, if necessary following consultation with other competent authorities, shall grant, subject to the criteria provided for in paragraph 2, the status of 'authorised economic operator' to any economic operator established in the customs territory of the Community. An authorised economic operator shall benefit from facilitations with regard to customs controls relating to security and safety and/or from simplifications provided for under the customs rules. The status of authorised economic operator shall, subject to the rules and conditions laid down in paragraph 2, be recognised by the customs

▼B

authorities in all Member States, without prejudice to customs controls. Customs authorities shall, on the basis of the recognition of the status of authorised economic operator and provided that the requirements relating to a specific type of simplification provided for in Community customs legislation are fulfilled, authorise the operator to benefit from that simplification.

2. The criteria for granting the status of authorised economic operator shall include:
   - an appropriate record of compliance with customs requirements,
   - a satisfactory system of managing commercial and, where appropriate, transport records, which allows appropriate customs controls,
   - where appropriate, proven financial solvency, and
   - where applicable, appropriate security and safety standards. The committee procedure shall be used to determine the rules:
   - for granting the status of authorised economic operator,
   - for granting authorisations for the use of simplifications,
   - for establishing which customs authority is competent to grant such status and authorisations,
   - for the type and extent of facilitations that may be granted in respect of customs controls relating to security and safety, taking into account the rules for common risk management,
   - for consultation with, and provision of information to, other customs authorities; and the conditions under which:
   - an authorisation may be limited to one or more Member States,
   - the status of authorised economic operator may be suspended or withdrawn, and
   - the requirement of being established in the Community may be waived for specific categories of authorised economic operator, taking into account, in particular, international agreements.

▼B

Section 2
Decisions relating to the application of customs rules

Article 6

1. Where a person requests that the customs authorities take a decision relating to the application of customs rules that person shall supply all the information and documents required by those authorities in order to take a decision.
2. Such decision shall be taken and notified to the applicant at the earliest opportunity.

Where a request for a decision is made in writing, the decision shall be made within a period laid down in accordance with the existing provisions, starting on the date on which the said request is received by the customs authorities. Such a decision must be notified in writing to the applicant.

However, that period may be exceeded where the customs authorities are unable to comply with it. In that case, those authorities shall so inform the applicant before the expiry of the abovementioned period, stating the grounds which justify exceeding it and indicating the further period of time which they consider necessary in order to give a ruling on the request.

3. Decisions adopted by the customs authorities in writing which either reject requests or are detrimental to the persons to whom they are addressed shall set out the grounds on which they are based. They shall refer to the right of appeal provided for in Article 243.
4. Provision may be made for the first sentence of paragraph 3 to apply likewise to other decisions.

Article 7

Save in the cases provided for in the second subparagraph of Article 244, decisions adopted shall be immediately enforceable by customs authorities.

Article 8

1. A decision favourable to the person concerned shall be annulled if it was issued on the basis of incorrect or incomplete information and:
   - the applicant knew or should reasonably have known that the information was incorrect or incomplete, and
   - such decision could not have been taken on the basis of correct or complete information.
2. The persons to whom the decision was addressed shall be notified of its annulment.
3. Annulment shall take effect from the date on which the annulled decision was taken.

Article 9

1. A decision favourable to the person concerned, shall be revoked or amended where, in cases other than those referred to in Article 8, one or more of the conditions laid down

for its issue were not or are no longer fulfilled.
2. A decision favourable to the person concerned may be revoked where the person to whom it is addressed fails to fulfil an obligation imposed on him under that decision.
3. The person to whom the decision is addressed shall be notified of its revocation or amendment.
4. The revocation or amendment of the decision shall take effect from the date of notification. However, in exceptional cases where the legitimate interests of the person to whom the decision is addresed so require, the customs authorities may defer the date when revocation or amendment takes effect.

Article 10

Articles 8 and 9 shall be without prejudice to national rules which stipulate that decisions are invalid or become null and void for reasons unconnected with customs legislation.
▼B

Section 3

Information

Article 11

1. Any person may request information concerning the application of customs legislation from the customs authorities. Such a request may be refused where it does not relate to an import or export operation actually envisaged.
2. The Information shall be supplied to the applicant free of charge. However, where special costs are incurred by the customs authorities, in particular as a result of analyses or expert reports on goods, or the return of the goods to the applicant, he may be charged the relevant amount.

▼M1

Article 12

1. The customs authorities shall issue binding tariff information or binding origin information on written request, acting in accordance with the committee procedure.
2. Binding tariff information or binding origin information shall be binding on the customs

authorities as against the holder of the information only in respect of the tariff classification or determination of the origin of goods. Binding tariff information or binding origin information shall be binding on the customs authorities only in respect of goods on which customs formalities are completed after the date on which the information was supplied by them. In matters of origin, the formalities in question shall be those relating to the application of Articles 22 and 27.

3. The holder of such information must be able to prove that:
   - for tariff purposes: the goods declared correspond in every respect to those described in the information,
   - for origin purposes: the goods concerned and the circumstances determining the acquisition of origin correspond in every respect to the goods and the circumstances described in the information.

4. Binding information shall be valid for a period of six years in the case of tariffs and three years in the case of origin from the date of issue. By way of derogation from Article 8, it shall be annulled where it is based on inaccurate or incomplete information from the applicant.

5. Binding information shall cease to be valid:
(a) in the case of tariff information:
   (i) where a regulation is adopted and the information no longer conforms to the law laid down thereby;
   (ii) where it is no longer compatible with the interpretation of one of the nomenclatures referred to in Article 20 (6):
      - at Community level, by reason of amendments to the explanatory notes to the combined nomenclature or by a judgment of the Court of Justice of the European Communities,
      - at international level, by reason of a classification opinion or an amendment of the explanatory notes to the Nomenclature of the Harmonized Commodity Description and Coding System, adopted by the World Customs Organi- zation established in 1952 under the name 'the Customs Cooperation Council';

▼B
   (iii) where it is revoked or amended in accordance with Article 9, provided that the

revocation or amendment is notified to the holder. The date on which binding information ceases to be valid for the cases cited in (i) and (ii)shall be the date of publication of the said measures or, in the case of international measures, the date of the Commission communication in the 'C' series of the Official Journal of the European Communities;

(b) in the case of origin information:
  (i) where a regulation is adopted or an agreement is concluded by the Community and the information no longer conforms to the law thereby laid down;
  (ii) where it is no longer compatible with:
    - at Community level, the explanatory notes and opinions adopted for the purposes of interpreting the rules or with a judgment of the Court of Justice of the European Communities,
    - at international level, the Agreement on Rules of Origin established in the World Trade Organization (WTO) or with the explanatory notes or an origin opinion adopted for the interpretation of that Agreement;
  (iii) where it is revoked or amended in accordance with Article 9, provided that the holder has been informed in advance. The date on which binding information ceases to be valid for the cases referred to in (i) and (ii) shall be the date indicated when the abovementioned measures are published or, in the case of international measures, the date shown in the Commission communication in the 'C' series of the Official Journal of the European Communities.

6. The holder of binding information which ceases to be valid ►C2 pursuant to paragraph 5 (a) (ii) or (iii) or (b) (ii) or (iii) ◄ may still use that information for a period of six months from the date of publication or notification, provided that he concluded binding contracts for the purchase or sale of the goods in question, on the basis of the binding information, before that measure was adopted. However, in the case of products for which an import, export or advance-fixing certificate is submitted when customs formalities are carried out, the period of six months is replaced by the period of validity of the certificate. In the case of paragraph 5 (a) (i) and b (i), the Regulation or agreement may lay down a period within which the first subparagraph shall apply.

7. The classification or determination of origin in binding information may by applied, on

the conditions laid down in paragraph 6, solely for the purpose of:
- determining import or export duties,
- calculating export refunds and any other amounts granted for imports or exports as part of the common agricultural policy,
- using import, export or advance-fixing certificates which are submitted when formalities are carried out for acceptance of the customs declaration concerning the goods in question, provided that such certificates were issued on the basis of the information concerned. In addition, in exceptional cases where the smooth operation of the arrangements laid down under the common agricultural policy may be ▼M1 jeopardized, it may be decided to derogate from paragraph 6, in accordance with the procedure laid down in Article 38 of Council Regulation No 136/66/EEC of 22 September 1966 on the establishment of a common organization of the market in oils and fats (1) and in the corresponding Articles in other regulations on the common organization of markets.
▼B

Section 4
Other provisions

▼M4

Article 13

1. Customs authorities may, in accordance with the conditions laid down by the provisions in force, carry out all the controls they deem necessary to ensure that customs rules and other legislation governing the entry, exit, transit, transfer and end-use of goods moved between the customs territory of the Community and third countries and the presence of goods that do not have Community status are correctly applied. Customs controls for the purpose of the correct application of Community legislation may be carried out in a third country where an international agreement provides for this.

2. Customs controls, other than spot-checks, shall be based on risk analysis using automated data processing techniques, with the purpose of identifying and quantifying the risks and developing the necessary measures to assess the risks, on the basis of

criteria developed at national, Community and, where available, international level. The committee procedure shall be used for determining a common risk management framework, and for establishing common criteria and priority control areas. Member States, in cooperation with the Commission, shall establish a computer system for the implementation of risk management.

3. Where controls are performed by authorities other than the customs authorities, such controls shall be performed in close coordination with the customs authorities, wherever possible at the same time and place.

4. In the context of the controls provided for in this Article, customs and other competent authorities, such as veterinary and police authorities, may communicate data received, in connection with the entry, exit, transit, transfer and end-use of goods moved between the customs territory of the Community and third countries and the presence of goods that do not have Community status, between each other and to the customs authorities of the Member States and to the Commission where this is required for the purposes of minimising risk. Communication of confidential data to the customs authorities and other bodies (e.g. security agencies) of third countries shall be allowed only in the framework of an international agreement and provided that the data protection provisions in force, in particular Directive 95/46/EC of the European Parliament and of the Council of 24 October 1995 on the protection of individuals with regard to the processing of personal data and on the free movement of such data (2) and Regulation (EC) No 45/2001 of the European Parliament and of the Council of 18 December 2000 on the protection of individuals with regard to the processing of personal data by the Community institutions and bodies and on the free movement of such data (3) are respected.

▼M1

(1) OJ No 172, 30.9.1966, p. 3025/66. Regulation as last amended by Regulation (EC) No 3290/94 (OJ No L 349, 31.12.1994, p. 105).

(2) OJ L 281, 23.11.1995, p. 31. Directive as amended by Regulation (EC) No 1882/2003 (OJ L 284, 31.10.2003, p. 1)

(3) OJ L 8, 12.1.2001, p. 1.

Article 14

For the purposes of applying customs legislation, any person directly or indirectly involved in the operations concerned for the purposes of trade in goods shall provide the customs authorities whith all the requisite documents and information, irrespective of the medium used, and all the requisite assistance at their request and by any time limit prescribed.

▼M4

Article 15

All information which is by nature confidential or which is provided on a confidential basis shall be covered by the duty of professional secrecy. It shall not be disclosed by the competent authorities without the express permission of the person or authority providing it. The communication of information shall, however, be permitted where the competent authorities are obliged to do so pursuant to the provisions in force, particularly in connection with legal proceedings. Any disclosure or communication of information shall fully comply with prevailing data protection provisions, in particular Directive 95/46/EC and Regulation (EC) No 45/2001.

▼B

Article 16

The persons concerned shall keep the documents referred to in Article 14 for the purposes of ►M4 customs controls ◄, for the period laid down in the provisions in force and for at least three calendar years, irrespective of the medium used. That period shall run from the end of the year in which:

(a) in the case of goods released for free circulation in circumstances other than those referred to in (b) or goods declared for export, from the end of the year in which the declarations for release for free circulation or export are accepted;

(b) in the case of goods released for free circulation at a reduced or zero rate of import duty on account of their end-use, from the end of the year in which they cease to be subject to customs supervision;

(c) in the case of goods placed under another customs procedure, from the end of the year in which the customs procedure concerned is completed;

(d) in the case of goods placed in a free zone or free warehouse, from the end of the year on which they leave the undertaking concerned. Without prejudice to the provisions of Article 221 (3), second sentence, where a check carried out by the customs authorities in respect of a customs debt shows that the relevant entry in the accounts has to be corrected, the documents shall be kept beyond the time limit provided for in the first paragraph for a period sufficient to permit the correction to be made and checked.

Article 17

Where a period, date or time limit is laid down pursuant to customs legislation for the purpose of applying legislation, such period shall not be extended and such date or time limit shall not be deferred unless specific provision is made in the legislation concerned.
▼M1

Article 18

1. The value of the ecu in national currencies to be applied for the purposes of determining the tariff classification of goods and import duties shall be fixed once a month. The rates to be used for this
▼B
conversion shall be those published in the Official Journal of the European Communities on the penultimate working day of the month. Those rates shall apply throughout the following month. However, where the rate applicable at the start of the month differs by more than 5 % from that published on the penultimate working day before the 15th of that same month, the latter rate shall apply from the 15th until the end of the month in question.
2. The value of the ecu in national currencies to be applied within the framework of customs legislation in cases other than those referred to in paragraph 1 shall be fixed once a year. The rates to be used for this conversion shall be those published in the Official Journal of the European Communities on the first working day of October, with effect from 1 January of the following year. If no rate is available for a particular national currency, the rate applicable to that currency shall be that obtaining on the last day for which a rate was published in the Official Journal of the European Communities.
3. The customs authorities may round up or down the sum resulting from the conversion into their national currency of an amount expressed in ecus for purposes other than determining the tariff classification of goods or import or export duties. The rounded-off

amount may not differ from the original amount by more than 5 %. The customs authorities may retain unchanged the national-currency value of an amount expressed in ecus if, at the time of the annual adjustment provided for in paragraph 2, the conversion of that amount, prior to the abovementioned rounding-off, results in a variation of less than 5 % in the national-currency value or a reduction in that value.

▼B

Article 19

The procedure of the Committee shall be used to determine in which cases and under which conditions the application of customs legislation may be simplified.

TITLE II
FACTORS ON THE BASIS OF WHICH IMPORT DUTIES ORPRESCRIBED IN RESPECT OF TRADE IN GOODS ARE APPLIED

CHAPTER 1
CUSTOMS TARIFF OF THE EUROPEAN COMMUNITIES AND TARIFF CLASSIFICATION OF GOODS

Article 20

1. Duties legally owed where a customs debt is incurred shall be based on the Customs Tariff of the European Communities.
2. The other measures prescribed by Community provisions governing specific fields relating to trade in goods shall, where appropriate, be applied according to the tariff classification of those goods.
3. The Customs Tariff of the European Communities shall comprise:
   (a) the combined nomenclature of goods;
   (b) any other nomenclature which is wholly or partly based on the combined nomenclature or which adds any subdivisions to it, and

▼M1

which is established by Community provisions governing specific fields with a view to the

application of tariff measures relating to trade in goods;
(c) the rates and other items of charge normally applicable to goods covered by the combined nomenclature as regards:
 - customs duties; and,
 - ►M1 _____ ◄ import charges laid down under the common agricultural policy or under the specific arrangements applicable to certain goods resulting from the processing of agricultural products.
(d) the preferential tariff measures contained in agreements which the Community has concluded with certain countries or groups of countries and which provide for the granting of preferential tariff treatment;
(e) preferential tariff measures adopted unilaterally by the Community in respect of certain countries, groups of countries or territories;
(f) autonomous suspensive measures providing for a reduction in or relief from import duties chargeable on certain goods;
(g) other tariff measures provided for by other Community legislation.
4. Without prejudice to the rules on flat-rate charges, the measures referred to in paragraph 3 (d), (e) and (f) shall apply at the declarant's request instead of those provided for in subparagraph (c) where the goods concerned fulfil the conditions laid down by those first mentioned measures. An application may be made after the event provided that the relevant conditions are fulfilled.
5. Where application of the measures referred to in paragraph 3 (d), (e) and (f) is restricted to a certain volume of imports, it shall cease: (a) in the case of tariff quotas, as soon as the stipulated limit on the volume of imports is reached; (b) in the case of tariff ceilings, by ruling of the Commission.
6. The tariff classification of goods shall be the determination, according to the rules in force, of:
 (a) the subheading of the combined nomenclature or the subheading of any other nomenclature referred to in paragraph 3 (b); or
 (b) the subheading of any other nomenclature which is wholly or partly based on the combined nomenclature or which adds any subdivisions to it, and which is established by Community provisions governing specific fields with a view to the

application of measures other than tariff measures relating to trade in goods, under which the aforesaid goods are to be classified.

Article 21

1. The favourable tariff treatment from which certain goods may benefit by reason of their nature or end-use shall be subject to conditions laid down in accordance with the committee procedure. Where an authorization is required Articles 86 and 87 shall apply.
2. For the purposes of paragraph 1, the expression 'favourable tariff treatment' means a reduction in or suspension of an import duty as referred to in Article 4 (10), even within the framework of a tariff quota.

▼B

CHAPTER 2
ORIGIN OF GOODS

Section 1
Non-preferential origin

Article 22

Articles 23 to 26 define the non-preferential origin of goods for the purposes of:
(a) applying the Customs Tariff of the European Communities with the exception of the measures referred to in Article 20 (3) (d) and (e);
(b) applying measures other than tariff measures established by Community provisions governing specific fields relating to trade in goods;
(c) the preparation and issue of certificates of origin.

Article 23

1. Goods originating in a country shall be those wholly obtained or produced in that country.
2. The expression 'goods wholly obtained in a country' means:
   (a) mineral products extracted within that country;

(b) vegetable products harvested therein;
(c) live animals born and raised therein;
(d) products derived from live animals raised therein;
(e) products of hunting or fishing carried on therein;
(f) products of sea-fishing and other products taken from the sea outside a country's territorial sea by vessels registered or recorded in the country concerned and flying the flag of that country;
(g) goods obtained or produced on board factory ships from the products referred to in subparagraph (f) originating in that country, provided that such factory ships are registered or recorded in that country and fly its flag;
(h) products taken from the seabed or subsoil beneath the seabed outside the territorial sea provided that country has exclusive rights to exploit that seabed or subsoil;
(i) waste and scrap products derived from manufacturing operations and used articles, if they were collected therein and are fit only for the recovery of raw materials;
(j) goods which are produced therein exclusively from goods referred to in sub paragraphs (a) to (i) or from their derivatives, at any stage of production.
3. For the purposes of paragraph 2 the expression 'country' covers that country's territorial sea.

Article 24

Goods whose production involved more than one country shall be deemed to originate in the country where they underwent their last, substantial, economically justified processing or working in an undertaking equipped for that purpose and resulting in the manufacture of a new product or representing an important stage of manufacture.

▼B

Article 25

Any processing or working in respect of which it is established, or in respect of which the facts as ascertained justify the presumption, that its sole object was to circumvent the provisions applicable in the Community to goods from specific countries shall under no circumstances be deemed to confer on the goods thus produced the origin of the country where it is carried out within the meaning of Article 24.

Article 26

1. Customs legislation or other Community legislation governing specific fields may provide that a document must be produced as proof of the origin of goods.
2. Notwithstanding the production of that document, the customs authorities may, in the event of serious doubts, require any additional proof to ensure that the indication of origin does comply with the rules laid down by the relevant Community legislation.

Section 2

Preferential origin of goods

Article 27

The rules on preferential origin shall lay down the conditions governing acquisition of origin which goods must fulfil in order to benefit from the measures referred to in Article 20(3)(d)or (e).

Those rules shall:

(a) in the case of goods covered by the agreements referred to in Article 20 (3) (d), be determined in those agreements;

(b) in the case of goods benefitting from the preferential tariff measures referred to in Article 20 (3) (e), be determined in accordance with the committee procedure.

CHAPTER 3

VALUE OF GOODS FOR CUSTOMS PURPOSES

Article 28

The provisions of this Chapter shall determine the customs value for the purposes of applying the Customs Tariff of the European Communities and non-tariff measures laid down by Community provisions governing specific fields relating to trade in goods.

Article 29

1. The customs value of imported goods shall be the transaction value, that is, the price actually paid or payable for the goods when sold for export to the customs territory of the Community, adjusted, where necessary, in accordance with Articles 32 and 33, provided:

    (a) that there are no restrictions as to the disposal or use of the goods by the buyer, other than restrictions which:
    - are imposed or required by a law or by the public authorities in the Community,
    - limit the geographical area in which the goods may be resold, or
    - do not substantially affect the value of the goods;

▼B

    (b) that the sale or price is not subject to some condition or consideration for which a value cannot be determined with respect to the goods being valued;
    (c) that no part of the proceeds of any subsequent resale, disposal or use of the goods by the buyer will accrue directly or indirectly to the seller, unless an appropriate adjustment can be made in accordance with Article 32; and
    (d) that the buyer and seller are not related, or, where the buyer and seller are related, that the transaction value is acceptable for customs purposes under paragraph 2.

2. (a) In determining whether the transaction value is acceptable for the purposes of paragraph 1, the fact that the buyer and the seller are related shall not in itself be sufficient grounds for regarding the transaction value as unacceptable. Where necessary, the circumstances surrounding the sale shall be examined and the transaction value shall be accepted provided that the relationship did not influence the price. If, in the light of information provided by the declarant or otherwise, the customs authorities have grounds for considering that the relationship influenced the price, they shall communicate their grounds to the declarant and he shall be given a reasonable opportunity to respond. If the declarant so requests, the communication of the grounds shall be in writing.

    (b) In a sale between related persons, the transaction value shall be accepted and the goods valued in accordance with paragraph 1 wherever the declarant demonstrates that such value closely approximates to one of the following occurring at or about the same time:

(i) the transaction value in sales, between buyers and sellers who ar not related in any particular case, of identical or similar goods for export to the Community;

(ii) the customs value of identical or similar goods, as determined under Article 30 (2) (c);

(iii) the customs value of identical or similar goods, as determined under Article 30 (2) (d). In applying the foregoing tests, due account shall be taken of demonstrated differences in commercial levels, quantity levels, the elements enumerated in Article 32 and costs incurred by the seller in sales in which he and the buyer are not related and where such costs are not incurred by the seller in sales in which he and the buyer are related.

(c) The tests set forth in subparagraph (b) are to be used at the initiative of the declarant and only for comparison purposes. Substitute values may not be established under the said subparagraph.

3. (a) The price actually paid or payable is the total payment made or to be made by the buyer to or for the benefit of the seller for the imported goods and includes all payments made or to be made as a condition of sale of the imported goods by the buyer to the seller or by the buyer to a third party to satisfy an obligation of the seller. The payment need not necessarily take the form of a transfer of money. Payment may be made by way of letters of credit or negotiable instrument and may be made directly or indirectly.

(b) Activities, including marketing activities, undertaken by the buyer on his own account, other than those for which an adjustment is provided in Article 32, are not considered to be an indirect payment to the seller, even though they might be regarded as of benefit to the seller or have been undertaken by

▼B

agreement with the seller, and their cost shall not be added to the price actually paid or payable in determining the customs value of imported goods.

Article 30

1. Where the customs value cannot be determined under Article 29, it is to be determined

by proceeding sequentially through sub paragraphs (a), (b), (c) and (d) of paragraph 2 to the first subparagraph under which it can be determined, subject to the proviso that the order of application of subparagraphs (c) and (d) shall be reversed if the declarant so requests; it is only when such value cannot be determined under a particular subparagraph that the provisions of the next subparagraph in a sequence established by virtue of this paragraph can be applied.

2. The customs value as determined under this Article shall be: (a) the transaction value of identical goods sold for export to the Community and exported at or about the same time as the goods being valued;

   (b) the transaction value of similar goods sold for export to the Community and exported at or about the same time as the goods being valued;

   (c) the value based on the unit price at which the imported goods for identical or similar imported goods are sold within the Community in the greatest aggregate quantity to persons not related to the sellers;

   (d) the computed value, consisting of the sum of:
   - the cost or value of materials and fabrication or other processing employed in producing the imported goods,
   - an amount for profit and general expenses equal to that usually reflected in sales of goods of the same class or kind as the goods being valued which are made by producers in the country of exportation for export to the Community,
   - the cost or value of the items referred to in Article 32 (1) (e).

3. Any further conditions and rules for the application of paragraph 2 above shall be determined in accordance with the committee procedure.

Article 31

1. Where the customs value of imported goods cannot be determined under Articles 29 or 30, it shall be determined, on the basis of data available in the Community, using reasonable means consistent with the principles and general provisions of:
   - the agreement on implementation of Article VII of the General Agreement on Tariffs and Trade ►M1 of 1994 ◄
   - Article VII of the General Agreement on Tariffs and Trade

►M1 of 1994 ◄

- the provisions of this chapter.

2. No customs value shall be determined under paragraph 1 on the basis of:
   (a) the selling price in the Community of goods produced in the Community;
   (b) a system which provides for the acceptance for customs purposes of the higher of two alternative values;
   (c) the price of goods on the domestic market of the country of exportation;

▼B

   (d) the cost of production, other than computed values which have been determined for identical or similar goods in accordance with Article 30 (2) (d);
   (e) prices for export to a country not forming part of the customs territory of the Community;
   (f) minimum customs values; or
   (g) arbitrary or fictitious values.

Article 32

1. In determining the customs value under Article 29, there shall be added to the price actually paid or payable for the imported goods:
   (a) the following, to the extent that they are incurred by the buyer but are not included in the price actually paid or payable for the goods:
      (i) commissions and brokerage, except buying commissions,
      (ii) the cost of containers which are treated as being one, for customs purposes, with the goods in question,
      (iii) the cost of packing, whether for labour or materials;
   (b) the value, apportioned as appropriate, of the following goods and services where supplied directly or indirectly by the buyer free of charge or at reduced cost for use in connection with the production and sale for export of the imported goods, to the extent that such value has not been included in the price actually paid or payable:
      (i) materials, components, parts and similar items incorporated in the imported goods,
      (ii) tools, dies, moulds and similar items used in the production of the imported goods,
      (iii) materials consumed in the production of the imported goods,

    (iv) engineering, development, artwork, design work, and plans and sketches undertaken elsewhere than in the Community and necessary for the production of the imported goods;
    (c) royalties and licence fees related to the goods being valued that the buyer must pay, either directly or indirectly, as a condition of sale of the goods being valued, to the extent that such royalties and fees are not included in the price actually paid or payable;
    (d) the value of any part of the proceeds of any subsequent resale, disposal or use of the imported goods that accrues directly or indirectly to the seller;
    (e) (i) the cost of transport and insurance of the imported goods, and (ii) loading and handling charges associated with the transport of the imported goods to the place of introduction into the customs territory of the Community.
2. Additions to the price actually paid or payable shall be made under this Article only on the basis of objective and quantifiable data.
3. No additions shall be made to the price actually paid or payable in determining the customs value except as provided in this Article.
4. In this Chapter, the term 'buying commissions' means fees paid by an importer to his agent for the service of representing him in the purchase of the goods being valued.
5. Notwithstanding paragraph 1 (c):

▼B
    (a) charges for the right to reproduce the imported goods in the Community shall not be added to the price actually paid or payable for the imported goods in determining the customs value; and
    (b) payments made by the buyer for the right to distribute or resell the imported goods shall not be added to the price actually paid or payable for the imported goods if such payments are not acondition of the sale for export to the Community of the goods.

Article 33

1. Provided that they are shown separately from the price actually paid or payable, the following shall not be included in the customs value:

(a) charges for the transport of goods after their arrival at the place of introduction into the customs territory of the Community;

(b) charges for construction, erection, assembly, maintenance or technical assistance, undertaken after importation of imported goods such as industrial plant, machinery or equipment;

(c) charges for interest under a financing arrangement entered into by the buyer and relating to the purchase of imported goods, irrespective of whether the finance is provided by the seller or another person, provided that the financing arrangement has been made in writing and where required, the buyer can demonstrate that:

- such goods are actually sold at the price declared as the price actually paid or payable, and
- the claimed rate of interest does not exceed the level for such transactions prevailing in the country where, and at the time when, the finance was provided;

(d) charges for the right to reproduce imported goods in the Community;

(e) buying commissions;

(f) import duties or other charges payable in the Community by reason of the importation or sale of the goods.

Article 34

Specific rules may be laid down in accordance with the procedure of the committee to determine the customs value of carrier media for use in data processing equipment and bearing data or instructions.

Article 35

▼M3

Where factors used to determine the customs value of goods are expressed in a currency other than that of the Member State where the valuation is made, the rate of exchange to be used shall be that duly published by the authorities competent in the matter.

▼B

Such rate shall reflect as effectively as possible the current value of such currency in commercial transactions in terms of the currency of such Member State and shall apply during such period as may be determined in accordance with the procedure of the committee. Where such a rate does not exist, the rate of exchange to be used shall be determined in accordance with the procedure of the committee.

▼B

Article 36

1. The provisions of this chapter shall be without prejudice to the specific provisions regarding the determination of the value for customs purposes of goods released for free circulation after being assigned a different customs-approved treatment or use.
2. By way of derogation from Articles 29, 30 and 31, the customs value of perishable goods usually delivered on consignment may, at the request of the declarant, be determined under simplified rules drawn up for the whole Community in accordance with the committee procedure.

TITLE III
PROVISIONS APPLICABLE TO GOODS BROUGHT INTO THE CUSTOMS TERRITORY OF THE COMMUNITY UNTIL THEY ARE ASSIGNED A CUSTOMS-APPROVED TREATMENT OR USE

CHAPTER 1
ENTRY OF GOODS INTO THE CUSTOMS TERRITORY OF THE COMMUNITY

▼M4

Article 36a

1. Goods brought into the customs territory of the Community shall be covered by a summary declaration, with the exception of goods carried on means of transport only passing through the territorial waters or the airspace of the customs territory without a stop within this territory.
2. The summary declaration shall be lodged at the customs office of entry. Customs authorities may allow the summary declaration to be lodged at another customs office,

provided that this office immediately communicates or makes available electronically the necessary particulars to the customs office of entry. Customs authorities may accept, instead of the lodging of the summary declaration, the lodging of a notification and access to the summary declaration data in the economic operator's computer system.
3. The summary declaration shall be lodged before the goods are brought into the customs territory of the Community.
4. The committee procedure shall be used to establish:
   - the time limit by which the summary declaration is to be lodged before the goods are brought into the customs territory of the Community,
   - the rules for exceptions from, and variations to, the time limit referred to in the first indent, and
   - the conditions under which the requirement for a summary declaration may be waived or adapted, in accordance with the specific circumstances and for particular types of goods traffic, modes of transport and economic operators and where international agreements provide for special security arrangements.

Article 36b

1. The committee procedure shall be used to establish a common data set and format for the summary declaration, containing the particulars necessary for risk analysis and the proper application of customs

▼B

controls, primarily for security and safety purposes, using, where appropriate, international standards and commercial practices.
2. The summary declaration shall be made using a data processing technique. Commercial, port or transport information may be used, provided that it contains the necessary particulars. Customs authorities may accept paper-based summary declarations in exceptional circumstances, provided that they apply the same level of risk management as that applied to summary declarations made using a data processing technique.
3. The summary declaration shall be lodged by the person who brings the goods, or who assumes responsibility for the carriage of the goods into the customs territory of the Community.

4. Notwithstanding the obligation of the person referred to in paragraph 3, the summary declaration may be lodged instead by:
   (a) the person in whose name the person referred to in paragraph 3 acts; or
   (b) any person who is able to present the goods in question or to have them presented to the competent customs authority; or
   (c) a representative of one of the persons referred to in paragraph 3 or points (a) or (b).
5. The person referred to in paragraphs 3 and 4 shall, at his request, be authorised to amend one or more particulars of the summary declaration after it has been lodged. However, no amendment shall be possible after the customs authorities:
   (a) have informed the person who lodged the summary declaration that they intend to examine the goods; or
   (b) have established that the particulars in questions are incorrect; or
   (c) have allowed the removal of the goods.

Article 36c

1. The customs office of entry may waive the lodging of a summary declaration in respect of goods for which, before expiry of the time limit referred to in Article 36a(3) or (4), a customs declaration is lodged. In such case, the customs declaration shall contain at least the particulars necessary for a summary declaration and, until such time as the former is accepted in accordance with Article 63, it shall have the status of a summary declaration. Customs authorities may allow the customs declaration to be lodged at a customs office of import different from the customs office of entry, provided that this office immediately communicates or makes available electronically the necessary particulars to the customs office of entry.
2. Where the customs declaration is lodged other than by use of data processing technique, the customs authorities shall apply the same level of risk management to the data as that applied to customs declarations made using a data processing technique.
▼B

Article 37

1. Goods brought into the customs territory of the Community shall, from the time of their entry, be subject to customs supervision. They may be subject to ►M4 customs controls

◄ in accordance with the provisions in force.
2. They shall remain under such supervision for as long as necessary to determine their customs status, if appropriate, and in the case of non-
▼M4
Community goods and without prejudice to Article 82 (1), until their customs status is changed, they enter a free zone or free warehouse or they are re-exported or destroyed in accordance with Article 182.

Article 38

1. Goods brought into the customs territory of the Community shall be conveyed by the person bringing them into the Community without delay, by the route specified by the customs authorities and in accordance with their instructions, if any:
   (a) to the customs office designated by the customs authorities or to any other place designated or approved by those authorities; or,
   (b) to a free zone, if the goods are to be brought into that free zone direct:
   - by sea or air, or
   - by land without passing through another part of the customs territory of the Community, where the free zone adjoins the land frontier between a Member State and a third country.
2. Any person who assumes responsibility for the carriage of goods after they have been brought into the customs territory of the Community, inter alia as a result of transhipment, shall become responsible for compliance with the obligation laid down in paragraph 1.
3. Goods which, although still outside the customs territory of the Community, may be subject to ►M4 customs controls by ◄ a Member State under the provisions in force, as a result of inter alia an agreement concluded between that Member State and a third country, shall be treated in the same way as goods brought into the customs territory of the Community.
4. Paragraph 1 (a) shall not preclude implementation of any provisions in force with respect to tourist traffic, frontier traffic, postal traffic or traffic of negligible economic importance, on condition that customs supervision and customs control possibilities are

not thereby jeopardized.

▼M4

5. Paragraphs 1 to 4 and Articles 36a to 36c and 39 to 53 shall not apply to goods which temporarily leave the customs territory of the Community while moving between two points in that territory by sea or air, provided that the carriage is effected by a direct route and by regular air or shipping services without a stop outside the customs territory of the Community.

▼B

6. Paragraph 1 shall not apply to goods on board vessels or aircraft crossing the territorial sea or airspace of the Member States without having as their destination a port or airport situated in those Member States.

Article 39

1. Where, by reason of unforeseeable circumstances or force majeure, the obligation laid down in Article 38 (1) cannot be complied with, the person bound by that obligation or any other person acting in his place shall inform the customs authorities of the situation without delay. Where the unforeseeable circumstances or force majeure do not result in total loss of the goods, the customs authorities shall also be informed of their precise location.

2. Where, by reason of unforeseeable circumstances or force majeure, a vessel or aircraft covered by Article 38 (6) is forced to put into port or land temporarily in the customs territory of the Community and the

▼B

obligation laid down in Article 38 (1) cannot be complied with, the person bringing the vessel or aircraft into the customs territory of the Community or any other person acting in his place shall inform the customs authorities of the situation without delay.

3. The customs authorities shall determine the measures to be taken in order to permit customs supervision of the goods referred to in paragraph 1 as well as those on board a vessel or aircraft in the circumstances specified in paragraph 2 and to ensure, where appropriate, that they are subsequently conveyed to a customs office or other place designated or approved by the authorities.

CHAPTER 2

PRESENTATION OF GOODS TO CUSTOMS

▼M4

Article 40

Goods entering the customs territory of the Community shall be presented to customs by the person who brings them into that territory or, if appropriate, by the person who assumes responsibility for carriage of the goods following such entry, with the exception of goods carried on means of transport only passing through the territorial waters or the airspace of the customs territory of the Community without a stop within this territory. The person presenting the goods shall make a reference to the summary declaration or customs declaration previously lodged in respect of the goods.

▼B

Article 41

Article 40 shall not preclude the implementation of rules in force relating to goods:

(a) carried by travellers;

(b) placed under a customs procedure but not presented to customs.

Article 42

Goods may, once they have been presented to customs, and with the permission of the customs authorities, be examined or samples may be taken, in order that they may be assigned a customs-approved treatment or use. Such permission shall be granted, on request, to the person authorized to assign the goods such treatment or use.

CHAPTER 3

UNLOADING OF GOODS PRESENTED TO CUSTOMS

▼B

Article 46

1. Goods shall be unloaded or transhipped from the means of transport carrying them solely with the permission of the customs authorities in places designated or approved

by those customs authorities. However, such permission shall not be required in the event of the imminent danger necessitating the immediate unloading of all or part of the goods. In that case, the customs authorities shall be informed accordingly forthwith.

▼B

2. For the purpose of inspecting goods and the means of transport carrying them, the customs authorities may at any time require goods to be unloaded and unpacked.

Article 47

Goods shall not be removed from their original position without the permission of the customs authorities.

CHAPTER 4
OBLIGATION TO ASSIGN GOODS PRESENTED TO CUSTOMS A CUSTOMS-APPROVED TREATMENT OR USE

Article 48

Non-Community goods presented to customs shall be assigned a customs-approved treatment or use authorized for such non- Community goods.

Article 49

1. Where goods are covered by a summary declaration, the formalities necessary for them to be assigned a customs-approved treatment or use must be carried out within:
    (a) 45 days from the date on which the summary declaration is lodged in the case of goods carried by sea;
    (b) 20 days from the date on which the summary declaration is lodged in the case of goods carried otherwise than by sea.
2. Where circumstances so warrant, the customs authorities may set a shorter period or authorize an extension of the periods referred to in paragraph 1. Such extension shall not, however, exceed the genuine requirements which are justified by the circumstances.

CHAPTER 5

TEMPORARY STORAGE OF GOODS

Article 50

Until such time as they are assignated a customs-approved treatment or use, goods presented to customs shall, following such presentation, have the status of goods in temporary storage. Such goods shall hereinafter be described as 'goods in temporary storage'.

Article 51

1. Goods in temporary storage shall be stored only in places approved by the customs authorities under the conditions laid down by those authorities.
2. The customs authorities may require the person holding the goods to provide security with a view to ensuring payment of any customs debt which may arise under Articles 203 or 204.

Article 52

Without prejudice to the provisions of Article 42, goods in temporary storage shall be subject only to such forms of handling as are designed to ensure their preservation in an unaltered state without modifying their appearance or technical characteristics.
▼B

Article 53

1. The customs authorities shall without delay take all measures necessary, including the sale of the goods, to regularize the situation of goods in respect of which the formalities necessary for them to be assigned a customs-approved treatment or use are not initiated within the periods determined in accordance with Article 49.
2. The customs authorities may, at the risk and expense of the person holding them, have the goods in question transferrred to a special place, which is under their supervision, until the situation of the goods is regularized.

CHAPTER 6

PROVISIONS APPLICABLE TO NON-COMMUNITY GOODS WHICH HAVE MOVED UNDER A TRANSIT PROCEDURE

Article 54

Article 38, with the exception of paragraph 1 (a) thereof, and Articles 39 to 53 shall not apply when goods already placed under a transit procedure are brought into the customs territory of the Community.

Article 55

Once non-Community goods which have moved under a transit procedure reach their destination in the customs territory of the Community and have been presented to customs in accordance with the rules governing transit, Article ►M1 42 ◄ to 53 shall apply.

CHAPTER 7
OTHER PROVISIONS

Article 56

Where the circumstances so require, the customs authorities may have goods presented to customs destroyed. The customs authorities shall inform the holder of the goods accordingly. The costs of destroying the goods shall be borne by the holder.

Article 57

Where customs authorities find that goods have been brought unauthorized into the customs territory of the Community or have been withheld from customs surveillance, they shall take any measures necessary, including sale of the goods, in order to regularize their situation.

TITLE IV
CUSTOMS-APPROVED TREATMENT OR USE

CHAPTER 1
GENERAL

Article 58

1. Save as otherwise provided, goods may at any time, under the conditions laid down, be assigned any customs-approved treatment or

▼B

use irrespective of their nature or quantity, or their country of origin, consignment or destination.

2. Paragraph 1 shall not preclude the imposition of prohibitions or restrictions justified on grounds of public morality, public policy or public security, the protection of health and life of humans, animals or plants, the protection of national treasures possessing artistic, historic or archaeological value or the protection of industrial and commercial property.

CHAPTER 2
CUSTOMS PROCEDURES

Section 1
Placing of goods under a customs procedure

Article 59

1. All goods Intended to be placed under a customs procedure shall be covered by a declaration for that customs procedure.

2. Community goods declared for an export, outward processing, transit or customs warehousing procedure shall be subject to customs supervision from the time of acceptance of the customs declaration until such time as they leave the customs territory of the Community or are destroyed or the customs declaration is invalidated.

Article 60

Insofar as Community customs legislation lays down no rules on the matter, Member States shall determine the competence of the various customs offices situated in their territory, account being taken, where applicable, of the nature of the goods and the customs procedure under which they are to be placed.

Article 61

The customs declaration shall be made:

(a) in writing; or

(b) using a data-processing technique where provided for by provisions laid down in accordance with the committee procedure or where authorized by the customs authorities; or

(c) by means of a normal declaration or any other act whereby the holder of the goods expresses his wish to place them under a customs procedure, where such a possibility is provided for by the rules adopted in accordance with the committee procedure.

A. Declarations in writing
I. Normal procedure

Article 62

1. Declarations in writing shall be made on a form corresponding to the official specimen prescribed for that purpose. They shall be signed and contain all the particulars necessary for implementation of the provisions governing the customs procedure for which the goods are declared.

▼B

2. The declaration shall be accompanied by all the documents required for implementation of the provisions governing the customs procedure for which the goods are declared.

Article 63

Declarations which comply with the conditions laid down in Article 62 shall be accepted by the customs authorities immediately, provided that the goods to which they refer are presented to customs.

Article 64

1. Subject to Article 5, a customs declaration may be made by any person who is able to present the goods in question or to have them presented to the competent customs authority, together with all the documents which are required to be produced for the application of the rules governing the customs procedure in respect of which the goods were declared.
2. However,
   (a) where acceptance of a customs declaration imposes particular obligations on a specific person, the declaration must be made by that person or on his behalf;
   (b) the declarant must be established in the Community. However, the condition regarding establishment in the Community shall not apply to persons who:? make a declaration for transit or temporary importation;? declare goods on an occasional basis, provided that the customs authorities consider this to be justified.
3. Paragraph 2 (b) shall not preclude the application by the Member States of bilateral agreements concluded with third countries, or customary practices having similar effect, under which nationals of such countries may make customs declarations in the territory of the Member States in question, subject to reciprocity.

Article 65

The declaration shall, at his request, be authorized to amend one or more of the particulars of the declaration after it has been accepted by customs. The amendment shall not have the effect of rendering the declaration applicable to goods other than those it originally covered. However, no amendment shall be permitted where authorization is requested after the customs authorities:
(a) have informed the declarant that they intend to examine the goods; or,
(b) have established that the particulars in question are incorrect; or,
(c) have released the goods.

Article 66

1. The customs authorities shall, at the request of the declarant, invalidate a declaration

already accepted where the declarant furnishes proof that goods were declared in error for the customs procedure covered by that declaration or that, as a result of special circumstances, the placing of the goods under the customs procedure for which they were declared is no longer justified.

▼B

Nevertheless, where the customs authorities have informed the declarant of their intention to examine the goods, a request for invalidation of the declaration shall not be accepted until after the examination has taken place.

2. The declaration shall not be invalidated after the goods have been released, expect in cases defined in accordance with the committee procedure.
3. Invalidation of the declaration shall be without prejudice to theapplication of the penal provisions in force.

Article 67

Save as otherwise expressly provided, the date to be used for the purposes of all the provisions governing the customs procedure for which the goods are declared shall be the date of acceptance of the declaration by the customs authorities.

Article 68

For the verification of declarations which they have accepted, the customs authorities may:
(a) examine the documents covering the declaration and the documents accompanying it. The customs authorities may require the declarant to present other documents for the purpose of verifying the accuracy of the particulars contained in the declaration;
(b) examine the goods and take samples for analysis or for detailed examination.

Article 69

1. Transport of the goods to the places where they are to be examined and samples are to be taken, and all the handling necessitated by such examination or taking of samples, shall be carried out by or under the responsibility of the declarant. The costs incurred shall be borne by the declarant.
2. The declarant shall be entitled to be present when the goods are examined and when samples are taken. Where they deem it appropriate, the customs authorities shall require

the declarant to be present or represented when the goods are examined or samples are taken in order to provide them with the assistance necessary to facilitate such examination or taking of samples.

3. Provided that samples are taken in accordance with the provisions in force, the customs authorities shall not be liable for payment of any compensation in respect thereof but shall bear the costs of their analysis or examination.

Article 70

1. Where only part of the goods covered by a declaration are examined, the results of the partial examination shall be taken to apply to all the goods covered by that declaration. However, the declarant may request a further examination of the goods if he considers that the results of the partial examination are not valid as regards the remainder of the goods declared.
2. For the purposes of paragraph 1, where a declaration form covers two or more items, the particulars relating to each item shall be deemed to constitute a separate declaration.

▼B

Article 71

1. The results of verifying the declaration shall be used for the purposes of applying the provisions governing the customs procedure under which the goods are placed.
2. Where the declaration is not verified, the provisions referred to in paragraph 1 shall be applied on the basis of the particulars contained in the declaration.

Article 72

1. The customs authorities shall take the measures necessary to identify the goods where identification is required in order to ensure compliance with the conditions governing the customs procedure for which the said goods have been declared.
2. Means of identification affixed to the goods or means of transport shall be removed or destroyed only by the customs authorities or with their permission unless, as a result of unforeseeable circumstances or force majeure, their removal or destruction is essential to ensure the protection of the goods or means of transport.

Article 73

1. Without prejudice to Article 74, where the conditions for placing the goods under the procedure in question are fulfilled and provided the goods are not subject to any prohibitive or restrictive measures, the customs authorities shall release the goods as soon as the particulars in the declaration have been verified or accepted without verification. The same shall apply where such verification cannot be completed within a reasonable period of time and the goods are no longer required to be present for verification purposes.
2. All the goods covered by the same declaration shall be released at the same time. For the purposes of this paragraph, where a declaration form covers two or more items, the particulars relating to each item shall be deemed to constitute a separate declaration.

Article 74

1. Where acceptance of a customs declaration gives rise to a customs debt, the goods covered by the declaration shall not be released unless the customs debt has been paid or secured. However, without prejudice to paragraph 2, this provision shall not apply to the temporary importation procedure with partial relief from import duties.
2. Where, pursuant to the provisions governing the customs procedure for which the goods are declared, the customs authorities require the provision of a security, the said goods shall not be released for the customs procedure in question until such security is provided.

Article 75

Any necessary measures, including confiscation and sale, shall be taken to deal with goods which:

(a) cannot be released because ? it has not been possible to undertake or continue examination of the goods within the period pre-scribed by the customs authorities for reasons attributable to the declarant; or,

▼B

? the documents which must be produced before the goods can be placed under the customs procedure requested have not been produced; or, ? payments or security which should have been made or provided in respect of import duties or export duties, as the case may be, have not been made or provided within the period prescribed; or, ? they are subject to bans or restrictions;

(b) are not removed within a reasonable period after their release.

II. Simplified procedures

Article 76

1. In order to simplify completion of formalities and procedures as far as possible while ensuring that operations are conducted in a proper manner, the customs authorities shall, under conditions laid down in accordance with the committee procedure, grant permission for:
   (a) the declaration referred to in Article 62 to omit certain of the particulars referred to in paragraph 1 of that Article for some of the documents referred to in paragraph 2 of that Article not to be attached thereto;
   (b) a commercial or administrative document, accompanied by request for the goods to be placed under the customs procedure in question, to be lodged in place of the declaration referred to in Article 62;
   (c) the goods to be entered for the procedure in question by means of an entry in the records; in this case, the customs authorities may waive the requirement that the declarant presents the goods to customs. The simplified declaration, commercial or administrative document or entry in the records must contain at least the particulars necessary for identification of the goods. Where the goods are entered in the records, the date of such entry must be included.
2. Except in cases to be determined in accordance with the committee procedure, the declarant shall furnish a supplementary declaration which may be of a general, periodic or recapitulative nature.
3. Supplementary declarations and the simplified declarations referred to in subparagraphs 1 (a), (b) and (c), shall be deemed to constitute a single, indivisible instrument taking effect on the date of acceptance of the simplified declarations; in the cases referred to in subparagraph 1 (c), entry in the records shall have the same legal force as acceptance of the declaration referred to in Article 62.

4. Special simplified procedures for the Community transit procedure shall be laid down in accordance with the committee procedure.

B. Other declarations

Article 77

1. Where the customs declaration is made by means of a data-processing technique within the meaning of Article 61 (b), or by an oral declaration or any other act within the meaning of Article 61 ©, Articles 62 to 76 shall apply mutatis mutandis without prejudice to the principles set out therein.

▼M3

2. Where the customs declaration is made by means of a dataprocessing technique, the customs authorities may allow accompanying

▼B

documents referred to in Article 62(2) not to be lodged with the declaration. In this case the documents shall be kept at the customs authorities' disposal.

▼B

C. Post-clearance examination of declarations

Article 78

1. The customs authorities may, on their own initiative or at the request of the declarant, amend the declaration after release of the goods.
2. The customs authorities may, after releasing the goods and in order to satisfy themselves as to the accuracy of the particulars contained in the declaration, inspect the commercial documents and data relating to the import or export operations in respect of the goods concerned or to subsequent commercial operations involving those goods. Such inspections may be carried out at the premises of the declarant, of any other person directly or indirectly involved in the said operations in a business capacity or of any other person in possession of the said document and data for business purposes. Those authorities may also examine the goods where it is still possible for them to be

produced.

3. Where revision of the declaration or post-clearance examination indicates that the provisions governing the customs procedure concerned have been applied on the basis of incorrect or incomplete information, the customs authorities shall, in accordance with any provisions laid down, take the measures necessary to regularize the situation, taking account of the new information available to them.

Section 2
Release for free circulation

Article 79

Release for free circulation shall confer on non-Community goods the customs status of Community goods.

It shall entail application of commercial policy measures, completion of the other formalities laid down in respect of the importation of goods and the charging of any duties legally due.

Article 80

1. By way of derogation from Article 67, provided that the import duty chargeable on the goods is one of the duties referred to in the first indent of Article 4 (10) and that the rate of duty is reduced after the date of acceptance of the declaration for release for free circulation but before the goods are released, the declarant may request application of the more favourable rate.

2. Paragraph 1 shall not apply where it has not been possible to release the goods for reasons attributable to the declarant alone.

Article 81

Where a consignment is made up of goods falling within different tariff classifications, and dealing with each of those goods in accordance with its tariff classification for the purpose of drawing up the declaration would entail a burden of work and expense disproportionate to the import duties chargeable, the customs authorities may, at the request of the

declarant, agree that import duties be charged on the whole
▼M3
consignment on the basis of the tariff classification of the goods which are subject to the highest rate of import duty.

Article 82

1. Where goods are released for free circulation at a reduced or zero rate of duty on account of their end-use, they shall remain under customs supervision. Customs supervision shall end when the conditions laid down for granting such a reduced or zero rate of duty cease to apply, where the goods are exported or destroyed or where the use of the goods for purposes other than those laid down for the application of the reduced or zero rate of duty is permitted subject to payment of the duties due.
2. Articles 88 and 90 shall apply mutatis mutandis to the goods referred to in paragraph 1.

Article 83

Goods released for free circulation shall lose their customs status as Community goods where:
(a) the declaration for release for free circulation is invalidated after release ?M1 _____ ?, or
(b) the imported duties payable on those goods are repaid or remitted:
  - under the inward processing procedure in the form of the drawback system; or - in respect of defective goods or goods which fail to comply with the terms of the contract, pursuant to Article 238; or ? in situations of the type referred to in Article 239 where repayment or remission is conditional upon the goods being exported or re-exported or being assigned an equivalent customs-approved treatment or use.

Section 3

Suspensive arrangements and customs procedures with economic impact

A. Provisions common to several procedures

Article 84

1. In Articles 85 to 90:
  (a) where the term 'procedure' is used, it is understood as applying, in the case of non-Community goods, to the following arrangements:
    - external transit;
    - customs warehousing;
    - inward processing in the form of a system of suspension;
    - processing under customs control;
    - temporary importation;
  (b) where the term 'customs procedure with economic impact' is used, it is understood as applying to the following arrangements:
    - customs warehousing;
    - inward processing;

▼B

- processing under customs control;
- temporary importation;
- outward processing.

2. 'Import goods' means goods placed under a suspensive procedure and goods which, under the inward processing procedure in the form of the drawback system, have undergone the formalities for release for free circulation and the formalities provided for in Article 125.

3. 'Goods in the unaltered state' means import goods which, under the inward processing procedure or the procedures for processing under customs control, have undergone no form of processing.

Article 85

The use of any customs procedure with economic impact shall be conditional upon authorization being issued by the customs authorities.

Article 86

Without prejudice to the additional special conditions governing the procedure in question, the authorization referred to in Article 85 and that referred to in Article 100 (1) shall be granted only:
- to persons who offer every guarantee necessary for the proper conduct of the operations;
- where the customs authorities can supervise and monitor the procedure without having to introduce administrative arrangements disproportionate to the economic needs involved.

Article 87

1. The conditions under which the procedure in question is used shall be set out in the authorization.
2. The holder of the authorization shall notify the customs authorities of all factors arising after the authorization was granted which may influence its continuation or content.

▼M1

Article 87a

In the cases referred to in the second sentence of the first indent of Article 4 (7), any products or goods obtained from goods placed under a suspensive arrangement shall be considered as being placed under the same arrangement.

▼B

Article 88

The customs authorities may make the placing of goods under a suspensive arrangement conditional upon the provision of security in order to ensure that any customs debt which may be incurred in respect of those goods will be paid. Special provisions concerning the provision of security may be laid down in the context of a specific suspensive arrangement.

Article 89

1. A suspensive arrangement with economic impact shall be discharged when a new customs-approved treatment or use is assigned either to the goods placed under that arrangement or to compensating or processed products placed under it.

▼B

2. The customs authorities shall take all the measures necessary to regularize the position of goods in respect of which a procedure has not been discharged under the conditions prescribed.

Article 90

The rights and obligations of the holder of a customs procedure with economic impact may, on the conditions laid down by the customs authorities, be transferred successively to other persons who fulfil any conditions laid down in order to benefit from the procedure in question.

B. External transit

I. General provisions

Article 91

1. The external transit procedure shall allow the movement from one point to another within the customs territory of the Community of:

   (a) non-Community goods, without such goods being subject to import duties and other charges or to commercial policy measures;

▼M2

   (b) Community goods, in cases and on conditions determined in accordance with the committee procedure, in order to prevent products covered by or benefiting from export measures from either evading or benefiting unjustifiably from such measures.

▼B

2. Movement as referred to in paragraph 1 shall take place:

   (a) under the external Community transit procedure; or

(b) under cover of a TIR carnet (TIR Convention) provided that such movement:

   (1) began or is to end outside the Community; or

   (2) relates to consignments of goods which must be unloaded in the customs territory of the Community and which are conveyed with goods to be unloaded in a third country; or

   (3) is effected between two points in the Community through the territory of a third country;

(c) under cover of an ATA carnet ?M1 _____ ? used as a transit document; or

(d) under cover of the Rhine Manifest (Article 9 of the revised Convention for the Navigation of the Rhine); or

(e) under cover of the form 302 provided for in the Convention between the Parties to the North Atlantic Treaty regarding the Status of their Forces, signed in London on 19 June 1951; or

(f) by post (including parcel post).

3. The external transit procedure shall apply without prejudice to the specific provisions applicable to the movement of goods placed under a customs procedure with economic impact.

▼M2

Article 92

1. The external transit procedure shall end and the obligations of the holder shall be met when the goods placed under the procedure and the required documents are produced at the customs office of destination in accordance with the provisions of the procedure in question.

▼B

2. The customs authorities shall discharge the procedure when they are in a position to establish, on the basis of a comparison of the data available to the office of departure and those available to the customs office of destination, that the procedure has ended correctly.

▼B

II. Specific provisions relating to external Community transit

Article 93

The external Community transit procedure shall apply to goods passing through the territory of a third country only if:

(a) provision is made to that effect under an international agreement; or

(b) carriage through that country is effected under cover of a single transport document drawn up in the customs territory of the Community; in such case the operation of that procedure shall be suspended in the territory of the third country.

▼M2

Article 94

1. The principal shall provide a guarantee in order to ensure payment of any customs debt or other charges which may be incurred in respect of the goods.

2. The guarantee shall be either:

   (a) an individual guarantee covering a single transit operation; or

   (b) a comprehensive guarantee covering a number of transit operations where the principal has been authorised to use such a guarantee by the customs authorities of the Member State where he is established.

3. The authorisation referred to in paragraph 2(b) shall be granted only to persons who:

   (a) are established in the Community;

   (b) are regular users of Community transit procedures or who are known to the customs authorities to have the capacity to fulfil their obligations in relation to these procedures, and

   (c) have not committed serious or repeated offences against customs or tax laws.

4. Persons who satisfy the customs authorities that they meet higher standards of reliability may be authorised to use a comprehensive guarantee for a reduced amount or to have a guarantee waiver. The additional criteria for this authorisation shall include:

   (a) the correct use of the Community transit procedures during a given period;

   (b) cooperation with the customs authorities, and

   (c) in respect of the guarantee waiver, a good financial standing which is sufficient to fulfil the commitments of the said persons. The detailed rules for authorisations granted under this paragraph shall be determined in accordance with the committee procedure.

5. The guarantee waiver authorised in accordance with paragraph 4 shall not apply to external Community transit operations involving goods which, as determined in accordance with the committee procedure, are considered to present increased risks.

6. In line with the principles underlying paragraph 4, recourse to the comprehensive guarantee for a reduced amount may, in the case of external Community transit, be temporarily prohibited by the

▼M2

committee procedure as an exceptional measure in special circumstances.

7. In line with the principles underlying paragraph 4, recourse to the comprehensive guarantee may, in the case of external Community transit, be temporarily prohibited by the committee procedure in respect of goods which, under the comprehensive guarantee, have been identified as being subject to large-scale fraud.

Article 95

1. Except in cases to be determined where necessary in accordance with the committee procedure, no guarantee need be furnished for:
   (a) journeys by air;
   (b) the carriage of goods on the Rhine and the Rhine waterways;
   (c) carriage by pipeline;
   (d) operations carried out by the railway companies of the Member States.
2. The cases in which the furnishing of a guarantee in respect of the carriage of goods on waterways other than those referred to in paragraph (b) may be waived shall be determined in accordance with the committee procedure.

▼B

Article 96

1. The principal shall be the of under the external Community transit procedure. He shall be responsible for:
   (a) production of the goods intact at the customs office of destination by the prescribed

time limit and with due observance of the measures adopted by the customs authorities to ensure identification;

(b) observance of the provisions relating to the Community transit procedure.

2. Notwithstanding the principal's obligations under paragraph 1, a carrier or recipient of goods who accepts goods knowing that they are moving under Community transit shall also be responsible for production of the goods intact at the customs office of destination by the prescribed time limit and with due observance of the measures adopted by the customs authorities to ensure identification.

▼M2

Article 97

1. The detailed rules for the operation of the procedure and the exemptions shall be determined in accordance with the committee procedure.
2. Provided that the implementation of Community measures applying to goods is guaranteed:
   (a) Member States have the right, by bilateral or multilateral arrangement, to establish between themselves simplified procedures consistent with criteria to be set according to the circumstances and applying to certain types of goods traffic or specific undertakings;
   (b) each Member State shall have the right to establish simplified procedures in certain circumstances for goods not required to move in the territory of another Member State.
3. Simplified procedures established under paragraph 2 shall be communicated to the Commission.

▼M2

C. Customs warehouses

Article 98

1. The customs warehousing procedure shall allow the storage in a customs warehouse of:
   (a) non-Community goods, without such goods being subject to import duties or

commercial policy measures;
(b) Community goods, where Community legislation governing specific fields provides that their being placed in a customs warehouse shall attract the application of measures normally attaching to the export of such goods.
2. Customs warehouse means any place approved by and under the supervision of the customs authorities where goods may be stored under the conditions laid down.
3. Cases in which the goods referred to in paragraph 1 may be placed under the customs warehousing procedure without being stored in a customs warehouse shall be determined in accordance with the committee procedure.

Article 99

A customs warehouse may be either a public warehouse or a private warehouse.

'Public warehouse' means a customs warehouse available for use by any person for the warehousing of goods; 'private warehouse' means a customs warehouse reserved for the warehousing of goods by the ware house keeper. The warehousekeeper is the person authorized to operate the customs warehouse. The depositer shall be the person bound by the declaration placing the goods under the customs warehousing procedure or to whom the rights and obligations of such a person have been transferred.

Article 100

1. Operation of a customs warehouse shall be subject to the issue of an authorization by the customs authorities, unless the said authorities operate the customs warehouse themselves.
2. Any person wishing to operate a customs warehouse must make a request in writing containing the information required for granting the authorization, in particular demonstrating that an economic need for warehousing exists. The authorization shall lay down the conditions for operating the customs warehouse.
3. The authorization shall be issued only to persons established in the Community.

Article 101

The warehousekeeper shall be responsible for:
(a) ensuring that while the goods are In the customs warehouse they are not removed from

customs supervision;

(b) fulfilling the obligations that arise from the storage of goods covered by the customs warehousing procedure; and

▼B

(c) complying with the particular conditions specified in the authorization.

Article 102

1. By way of derogation from Article 101, where the authorization concerns a public warehouse, it may provide that the responsibilities referred to in Article 101 (a) and/or (b) devolve exclusively upon the depositor.
2. The depositor shall at all times be responsible for fulfilling the obligations arising from the placing of goods under the customs warehousing procedure.

Article 103

The rights and obligations of a warehousekeeper may, with the agreement of the customs authorities, be transferred to another person.

Article 104

Without prejudice to Article 88, the customs authorities may demand that the warehousekeeper provide a guarantee in connection with the responsibilities specified in Article 101.

Article 105

The person designated by the customs authorities shall keep stock records of all the goods placed under the customs warehousing procedure in a form approved by those authorities. Stock records are not necessary where a public warehouse is operated by the customs authorities. Subject to the application of Article 86 the customs authorities may dispense with stock records where the responsibilities referred to in Article 101 (a) and/or (b) lie exclusively with the depositor and the goods are placed under that procedure on the basis of a written declaration forming part of the normal procedure or an administrative document in accordance with Article 76 (1) (b).

Article 106

1. Where an economic need exists and customs supervision is not adversely affected thereby, the customs authorities may allow:
   (a) Community goods other than those referred to in Article 98 (1) (b) to be stored on the premises of a customs warehouse;
   (b) non-Community goods to be processed on the premises of a customs warehouse under the inward processing procedure, subject to the conditions provided for by that procedure. The formalities which may be dispensed with in a customs warehouse shall be determined in accordance with the committee procedure;
   (c) non-Community goods to be processed on the premises of a customs warehouse under the procedure for processing under customs control, subject to the conditions provided for by that procedure. The formalities which may be dispensed with in a customs warehouse shall be determined in accordance with the committee procedure.
2. In the cases referred to in paragraph 1, the goods shall not be subject to the customs warehousing procedure.
3. The customs authorities may require the goods referred to in paragraph 1 to be entered in the stock records provided for in Article 105.

▼B

Article 107

Goods placed under the customs warehousing procedure shall be entered in the stock records provided for in Article 105 as soon as they are brought into the customs warehouse.

Article 108

1. There shall be no limit to the length of time goods may remain under the customs warehousing procedure. However, in exceptional cases, the customs authorities may set a time limit by which the depositor must assign the goods a new customsapproved treatment or use.
2. Specific time limits for certain goods referred to in Article 98 (1) (b) covered by the common agricultural policy may be laid down in accordance with the committee

procedure.

Article 109

1. Import goods may undergo the usual forms of handling intended to preserve them, improve their appearance or marketable quality or prepare them for distribution or resale. A list of cases in which those forms of handling shall be prohibited for goods covered by the common agricultural policy may be drawn up if this is necessary to ensure the smooth operation of the common organization of markets.
2. Community goods referred to in Article 98 (1) (b) which are placed under the customs warehousing procedure and are covered by the common agricultural policy may undergo only the forms of handling expressly stipulated for such goods.
3. The forms of handling provided for in the first subparagraph of paragraph 1 and in paragraph 2 must be authorized in advance by the customs authorities, which shall lay down the conditions under which they may take place.
4. The lists of the forms of handling referred to in paragraphs 1 and 2 shall be established in accordance with the committee procedure.

Article 110

Where circumstances so warrant, goods placed under the customs warehousing procedure may be temporarily removed from the customs warehouse. Such removal must be authorized in advance by the customs authorities, who shall stipulate the conditions on which it may take place. While they are outside the customs warehouse the goods may undergo the forms of handling referred to in Article 109 on the conditions set out therein.

Article 111

The customs authorities may allow goods placed under the customs warehousing procedure to be transferred from one customs warehouse to another.

Article 112

1. Where a customs debt is incurred in respect of import goods and the customs value of such goods is based on a price actually paid or payable which includes the cost of warehousing and of preserving goods while they remain in the warehouse, such costs

need not be
▼B
included in the customs value if they are shown separately from the price actually paid or payable for the goods.
2. Where the said goods have undergone the usual forms of handling within the meaning of Article 109, the nature of the goods, the customs value and the quantity to be taken into account in determining the amount of import duties shall, at the request of the declarant, be those which would be taken into account for the goods, at the time referred to in Article 214, if they had not undergone such handling. However, derogations from this provision may be adopted under the committee procedure.
▼M1
3. Where import goods are released for free circulation in accordance with Article 76 (1) (c), the nature of the goods, the customs value and the quantity to be taken into account for the purposes of Article 214 shall be those applicable to the goods at the time when they were placed under the customs-warehousing procedure. The first subparagraph shall apply provided that the rules of assessment relating to those goods were ascertained or accepted at the time when the goods were placed under the customs-warehousing procedure, unless the declarant requests their application at the time when the customs debt is incurred. The first subparagraph shall apply without prejudice to a post-clearance examination within the meaning of Article 78.
▼B

Article 113

Community goods referred to in Article 98 (1) (b) which are covered by the common agricultural policy and are placed under the customs warehousing procedure must be exported or be assigned a treatment or use provided for by the Community legislation governing specific fields referred to in that Article.

D. Inward processing

I. General

Article 114

1. Without prejudice to Article 115, the inward processing procedure shall allow the following goods to be used in the customs territory of the Community in one or more processing operations:
    (a) non-Community goods intended for re-export from the customs territory of the Community in the form of compensating products, without such goods being subject to import duties or commercial policy measures;
    (b) goods released for free circulation with repayment or remission of the import duties chargeable on such goods if they are exported from the customs territory of the Community in the form of compensating products.
2. The following expressions shall have the following meanings:
    (a) suspension system: the inward processing relief arrangements as provided for in paragraph 1 (a);
    (b) drawback system: the inward processing relief arrangements as provided for in paragraph 1 (b);
    (c) processing operations: the working of goods, including erecting or assembling them or fitting them to other goods,

▼B
- the processing of goods, and
- the repair of goods, including restoring them and putting them in order;
- the use of certain goods defined in accordance with the committee procedure which are not to be found in the compensating products, but which allow or facilitate the production of those products, even if they are entirely or partially used up in the process;
    (d) compensating products: all products resulting from processing operations;
    (e) equivalent goods: Community goods which are used instead of the import goods for the manufacture of compensating products;
    (f) rate of yield: the quantity or percentage of compensating products obtained from the

processing of a given quantity of import goods.

Article 115

1. Where the conditions laid down in paragraph 2 are fulfilled, and subject to paragraph 4, the customs authorities shall allow:
   (a) compensating products to be obtained from equivalent goods;
   (b) compensating products obtained from equivalent goods to be exported from the Community before importation of the import goods.
2. Equivalent goods must be of the same quality and have the same characteristics as the import goods. However, in specific cases determined in accordance with the committee procedure, equivalent goods may be allowed to be at a more advanced stage of manufacture than the import goods.
3. Where paragraph 1 applies, the import goods shall be regarded for customs purposes as equivalent goods and the latter as import goods.

▼M3

4. Measures aimed at prohibiting, imposing certain conditions for or facilitating recourse to paragraph 1 may be adopted in accordance with the committee procedure.

▼B

5. Where paragraph 1 (b) is applied and the compensating products would be liable to export duties if they were not being exported or reexported under an inward processing operation, the holder of the authorization shall provide a security to ensure payment of the duties should the import goods not be imported within the period prescribed.

II. Grant of the authorization

Article 116

The authorization shall be issued at the request of the person who carries out processing operations or who arranges for them to be carried out.

Article 117

The authorization shall be granted only:

(a) to persons established in the Community. However, the authorization may be granted to persons established outside the Community in respect of imports of a non-commercial nature;

▼B

(b) where, without prejudice to the use of the goods referred to in the last indent of Article 114 (2) (c) final indent, the import goods can be identified in the compensating products or, in the case referred to in Article 115, where compliance with the conditions laid down in respect of equivalent goods can be verified;

(c) where the inward processing procedure can help create the most favourable conditions for the export or re-export of compensating products, provided that the essential interests of Community producers are not adversely affected (economic conditions).

▶M3 The cases in which the economic conditions are deemed to have been fulfilled may be determined in accordance with the committee procedure.

III. Operation of the procedure

Article 118

1. The customs authorities shall specify the period within which the compensating products must have been exported or re-exported or assigned another customs-approved treatment or use. That period shall take account of the time required to carry out the processing operations and dispose of the compensating products.

2. The period shall run from the date on which the non-Community goods are placed under the inward processing procedure. The customs authorities may grant an extension on submission of a duly substantiated request by the holder of the authorization. For reasons of simplification, it may be decided that a period which commences in the course of a calendar month or quarter shall end on the last day of a subsequent calendar month or quarter respectively.

3. Where Article 115 (1) (b) applies, the customs authorities shall specify the period within which the non-Community goods must be declared for the procedure. That period shall run from the date of acceptance of the export declaration, relating to the compensating products obtained from the corresponding equivalent goods.

4. Specific time limits may be laid down in accordance with the committee procedure for certain processing operations or for certain import goods.

Article 119

1. The customs authorities shall set either the rate of yield of the operation or where appropriate, the method of determining such rate. The rate of yield shall be determined on the basis of the actual circumstances in which the processing operation is, or is to be, carried out.
2. Where circumstances so warrant and, in particular, in the case of processing operation customarily carried out under clearly defined technical conditions involving goods of substantially uniform characteristics and resulting in the production of compensating products of uniform quality, standard rates of yield may be set in accordance with the committee procedure on the basis of actual data previously ascertained.

Article 120

The cases in which and the conditions under which goods in the unaltered state or compensating products shall be considered to have been released for free circulation may be determined in accordance with the committee procedure.

▼B

Article 121

1. Subject to Article 122, where a customs debt is incurred, the amount of such debt shall be determined on the basis of the taxation elements appropriate to the import goods at the time of acceptance of the declaration of placing of these goods under the inward processing procedure.
2. If at the time referred to in paragraph 1 the import goods fulfilled the conditions to quality for preferential tariff treatment within tariff quotas or ceilings, they shall be eligible for any preferential tariff treatment existing in respect of identical goods at the time of acceptance of the declaration of release for free circulation.

Article 122

By way of derogation from Article 121, compensating products:
(a) shall be subject to the import duties appropriate to them where:

- they are released for free circulation and appear on the list adopted in accordance with the committee procedure, to the extent that they are in proportion to the exported part of the compensating products not included in that list. However, the holder of the authorization may ask for the duty on those products to be assessed in the manual referred to in Article 121,
- they are subject to charges established under the common agricultural policy, and provisions adopted in accordance with the committee procedure so provide;

(b) shall be subject to import duties calculated in accordance with the rules applicable to the customs procedure in question or to free zones or free warehouses where they have been placed under a suspensive arrangement or in a free zone or free warehouse; However,-
- the person concerned may request that duty be assessed in accordance with Article 121;
- in cases where the compensating products have been assigned a customs-approved treatment or use referred to above other than processing under customs control, the amount of the import duty levied shall be at least equal to the amount calculated in accordance with Article 121;

(c) may be made subject to the rules governing assessment of duty laid down under the procedure for processing under customs control where the import goods could have been placed under that procedure;

(d) shall enjoy favourable tariff treatment owing to the special use for which they are intended, where provision is made for such treatment in the case of identical imported goods;

(e) shall be admitted free of import duty where such duty-free provision is made in the case of identical goods imported in accordance with Article 184.

IV. Processing operations outside the customs territory of the Community

Article 123

1. Some or all of the compensating products or goods in the unaltered state may be temporarily exported for the purpose of further processing outside the customs territory of the Community if the

▼B

customs authority so authorizes, in accordance with the conditions laid down in the outward processing provisions.

2. Where a customs debt is incurred in respect of reimported products, the following shall be charged:
   (a) import duties on the compensating products or goods in the unaltered state referred to in paragraph 1, calculated in accordance with Articles 121 and 122; and
   (b) import duties on products reimported after processing outside the customs territory of the Community, the amount of which shall be calculated in accordance with the provisions relating to the outward processing procedure, on the same conditions as would have applied had the products exported under the latter procedure been released for free circulation before such export took place.

V. Special provisions relating to the drawback system

▼M3

Article 124

1. The drawback system may be used for all goods. It shall not, however, be usable where, at the time the declaration of release for free circulation is accepted:
   - the import goods are subject to quantitative import restrictions,
   - a tariff measure within quotas is applied to the import goods,
   - the import goods are subject to presentation of an import or export licence or certificate in the framework of the common agricultural policy, or
   - an export refund or tax has been set for the compensating products.
2. Moreover, no reimbursement of import duties under the drawback system shall be possible if, at the time the export declaration for the compensating products is accepted, these products are subject to presentation of an import or export licence or certificate in the framework of the common agricultural policy or an export refund or tax has been set for them.
3. Derogations from paragraphs 1 and 2 may be laid down in accordance with the committee procedure.

▼B

Article 125

1. The declaration of release for free circulation shall indicate that the drawback system is being used and shall provide particulars of the authorization.
2. At the request of the customs authorities, the said authorization shall be attached to the declaration of release for free circulation.

Article 126

Under the drawback system, Article 115 (1) (b), (3) and (5), Article 118 (3), Articles 120 and 121, Article 122 (a), second indent, and (c), and Article 129 shall not apply.

Article 127

Temporary exportation of compensating products carried out as provided for in Article 123 (1) shall not be considered to be exportation within the meaning of Article 128 except where such products are not reimported into the Community within the period prescribed.

▼B

Article 128

▼M1

1. The holder of the authorization may ask for the import duty to be repaid or remitted where he can establish to the satisfaction of the customs authorities that import goods released for free circulation under the drawback system in the form of compensating products orgoods in the unaltered state have been either:

   - exported, or

   ▼B

   - placed, with a view to being subsequently re-exported, under the transit procedure, the customs-warehousing procedure, the temporary importation procedure or the inward-processing procedure (suspensive arrangement), or in a free zone or free warehouse, provided that all conditions for use of the procedure have also been fulfilled.

2. For the purposes of being assigned a customs-approved treatment or use referred to in the second indent of paragraph 1, compensating products or goods in the unaltered

state shall be considered to be non- Community goods.
3. The period within which the application for repayment must be made shall be determined in accordance with the committee procedure.

▼M1
4. Without prejudice to point (b) of Article 122, where compensating products or goods in the unaltered state placed under a customs procedure or in a free zone or free warehouse in accordance with paragraph 1 are released for free circulation, the amount of import duties repaid or remitted shall be considered to constitute the amount of the customs debt.

▼B
5. For the purpose of determining the amount of import duties to be repaid or remitted, the first indent of Article 122 (a) shall apply mutatis mutandis.

VI. Other provisions

Article 129

The inward processing procedure, applying the suspension system shall also apply in order that the compensating products may qualify for exemption from the export duties to which identical products obtained from Community goods instead of import goods would be liable.

E. Processing under customs control

Article 130

The procedure for processing under customs control shall allow non- Community goods to be used in the customs territory of the Community in operations which alter their nature or state, without their being subject to import duties or commercial policy measures, and shall allow the products resulting from such operations to be released for free circulation at the rate of import duty appropriate to them. Such products shall be termed processed products.

▼B

Article 131

The cases in and specific conditions under which the procedure for processing under customs control may be used shall be determined in accordance with the committee procedure.

▼B

Article 132

Authorization for processing under customs control shall be granted at the request of the person who carries out the processing or arranges for it to be carried out.

Article 133

Authorization shall be granted only:

(a) to persons established in the Community;

(b) where the import goods can be identified in the processed products;

(c) where the goods cannot be economically restored after processing to their description or state as it was when they were placed under the procedure;

(d) where use of the procedure cannot result in circumvention of the effect of the rules concerning origin and quantitative restrictions applicable to the imported goods;

(e) where the necessary conditions for the procedure to help create or maintain a processing activity in the Community without adversely

affecting the essential interests of Community producers of similar goods (economic conditions) are fulfilled. ?M3 The cases in which the economic conditions are deemed to have been fulfilled may be determined in accordance with the committee procedure.

Article 134

Article 118 (1), (2) and (4) and Article 119 shall apply mutatis mutandis.

Article 135

Where a customs debt is incurred in respect of goods in the unaltered state or of products that are at an intermediate stage of processing as compared with that provided for in the authorization, the amount of that debt shall be determined on the basis of the items of charge elements appropriate to the import goods at the time of acceptance of the declaration relating to the placing of the goods under the procedure for processing under customs control.

Article 136

1. Where the import goods qualified for preferential tariff treatment when they were placed under the procedure for processing under customs control, and such preferential tariff treatment is applicable to products identical to the processed products released for free circulation, the import duties to which the processed products are subject shall be calculated by applying the rate of duty applicable under that treatment.
2. If the preferential tariff treatment referred to in paragraph 1 in respect of the import goods is subject to tariff quotas or tariff ceilings, the application of the rate of duty referred to in paragraph 1 in respect of the processed products shall also be subject to the condition that the said preferential tariff treatment is applicable to the import goods at the time of acceptance of the declaration of release for free circulation. In this case, the quantity of import goods actually used in the manufacture of the processed products released for free circu-

▼M3

lation shall be charged against the tariff quotas or ceilings in force at the time of acceptance of the declaration of release for free circulation and no quantities shall be counted against tariff quotas or ceilings opened in respect of products identical to the processed products.

F. Temporary importation

Article 137

The temporary importation procedure shall allow the use in the customs territory of the Community, with total or partial relief from import duties and without their being subject to commercial policy measures, of non-Community goods intended for re-export without having undergone any change except normal depreciation due to the use made of them.

Article 138

Authorization for temporary importation shall be granted at the request of the person who uses the goods or arranges for them to be used.

Article 139

The customs authorities shall refuse to authorize use of the temporary importation procedure where it is impossible to ensure that the import goods can be identified. However, the customs authorities may authorize use of the temporary importation procedure without ensuring that the goods can be identified where, in view of the nature of the goods or of the operations to be carried out, the absence of identification measures is not liable to give rise to any abuse of the procedure.

Article 140

1. The customs authorities shall determine the period within which import goods must have been re-exported or assigned a new customsapproved treatment or use. Such period must be long enough for the objective of authorized use to be achieved.
2. Without prejudice to the special periods laid down in accordance with Article 141, the maximum period during which goods may remain under the temporary importation procedure shall be 24 months. The customs authorities may, however, determine shorter periods with the agreement of the person concerned.
3. However, where exceptional circumstances so warrant, the customs authorities may, at the request of the person concerned and within reasonable limits, extend the periods referred to in paragraphs 1 and 2 in order to permit the authorized use.

Article 141

The case and the special conditions under which the temporary importation procedure may be used with total relief from import duties shall be determined in accordance with the committee procedure.

▼M3

Article 142

1. Use of the temporary importation procedure with partial relief from import duties shall be granted in respect of goods which are not covered by the provisions adopted in accordance with Article 141 or which are covered by such provisions but do not fulfil all

the conditions

▼B

laid down therein for the grant of temporary importation with total relief.

2. The list of goods in respect of which the temporary importation procedure with partial relief from import duties may not be used and the conditions subject to which the procedure may be used shall be determined in accordance with the committee procedure.

▼B

Article 143

1. The amount of import duties payable in respect of goods placed under the temporary importation procedure with partial relief from import duties shall be set at 3%, for every month or fraction of a month during which the goods have been placed under the temporary importation procedure with partial relief, of the amount of duties which would have been payable on the said goods had they been released for free circulation on the date on which they were placed under the temporary importation procedure.

2. The amount of import duties to be charged shall not exceed that which would have been charged if the goods concerned had been released for free circulation on the date on which they were placed under the temporary importation procedure, leaving out of account any interest which may be applicable.

3. Transfer of the rights and obligations deriving from the temporary importation procedure pursuant to Article 90 shall not mean that the same relief arrangements must be applied to each of the periods of use to be taken into consideration.

4. Where the transfer referred to in paragraph 3 is made with partial relief for both persons authorized to use the procedure during the same month, the holder of the initial authorization shall be liable to pay the amount of import duties due for the whole of that month.

Article 144

1. Where a customs debt is incurred in respect of import goods, the amount of such debt shall be determined on the basis of the taxation elements appropriate to those goods at the time of acceptance of the declaration of their placing under the temporary

importation procedure. However, where the provisions of Article 141 so provide, the amount of the debt shall be determined on the basis of the taxation elements appropriate to the goods in question at the time referred to in Article 214.

2. Where, for a reason other than the placing of goods under the temporary importation procedure with partial relief from import duties, a customs debt is incurred in respect of goods placed under the said procedure, the amount of that debt shall be equal to the difference between the amount of duties calculated pursuant to paragraph 1 and that payable pursuant to Article 143.

G. Outward processing

I. General

Article 145

1. The outward processing procedure shall, without prejudice to the provisions governing specific fields relating to the standard exchange system laid down in Articles 154 to 159 or to Article 123, allow Community goods to be exported temporarily from the customs territory of the Community in order to undergo processing operations

▼M3

and the products resulting from those operations to be released for free circulation with total or partial relief from import duties.

2. Temporary exportation of Community goods shall entail the application of export duties, commercial policy measures and other formalities for the exit of Community goods from the customs territory of the Community.

3. The following definitions shall apply:
   (a) 'temporary export goods' means goods placed under the outward processing procedure;
   (b) 'processing operations' means the operations referred to in Article 114 (2) (c), first, second and third indents;
   (c) 4'compensating products' means all products resulting from processing operations;
   (d) 'rate of yield' means the quantity or percentage of compensating products obtained

from the processing of a given quantity of temporary export goods.

Article 146

1. The outward processing procedure shall not be open to Community goods:
   - whose export gives rise to repayment or remission of import duties,
   - which, prior to export, were released for free circulation with total relief from import duties by virtue of end use, for as long as the conditions for granting such relief continue to apply,
   - whose export gives rise to the granting of export refunds or in respect of which a financial advantage other than such refunds is granted under the common agricultural policy by virtue of the export of the said goods.
2. However, derogations from the second indent of paragraph 1 may be determined in accordance with the committee procedure.

II. Grant of the authorization

Article 147

1. Authorization to use the outward processing procedure shall be issued at the request of the person who arranges for the processing operations to be carried out.
2. By way of derogation from paragraph 1, authorization to use the outward processing procedure may be granted to another person in respect of goods of Community origin within the meaning of Title II, Chapter 2, Section 1, where the processing operation consists in incorporating those goods into goods obtained outside the Community and imported as compensating products, provided that use of the procedure helps to promote the sale of export goods without adversely affecting the essential interests of Community producers of products identical or similar to the imported compensating products. The cases in which and the arrangements under which the preceding subparagraph shall apply shall be determined in accordance with the committee procedure.

Article 148

Authorization shall be granted only:

(a) to persons established in the Community;

▼B

(b) where it is considered that it will be possible to establish that the compensating products have resulted from processing of the temporary export goods. The cases in which derogations from this subparagraph may apply and the conditions under which such derogations shall apply shall be determined in accordance with the committee procedure;

(c) where authorization to use the outward processing procedure is not liable seriously to harm the essential interests of Community processors (economic conditions).

III. Operation of the procedure

Article 149

1. The customs authorities shall specify the period within which the compensating products must be reimported into the customs territory of the Community. They may extend that period on submission of a duly substantiated request by the holder of the authorization.

2. The customs authorities shall set either the rate of yield of the operation or, where necessary, the method of determining that rate.

Article 150

1. The total or partial relief from import duties provided for in Article 151 (1) shall be granted only where the compensating products are declared for release for free circulation in the name of or on behalf of:

    (a) the holder of the authorization, or

    (b) any other person established in the Community provided that that person has obtained the consent of the holder of the authorization and the conditions of the authorization are fulfilled.

2. The total or partial relief from import duties provided for in Article 151 shall not be

granted where one of the conditions or obligations relating to the outward processing procedure is not fulfilled, unless it is established that the failures have no significant effect on the correct operation of the said procedure.

Article 151

1. The total or partial relief from import duties provided for in Article 145 shall be effected by deducting from the amount of the import duties applicable to the compensating products released for free circulation the amount of the import duties that would be applicable on the same date to the temporary export goods if they were imported into the customs territory of the Community from the country in which they underwent the processing operation or last processing operation.
2. The amount to be deducted pursuant to paragraph 1 shall be calculated on the basis of the quantity and nature of the goods in question on the date of acceptance of the declaration placing them under the outward processing procedure and on the basis of the other items of charge applicable to them on the date of acceptance of the declaration relating to the release for free circulation of the compensating products. The value of the temporary export goods shall be that taken into account for those goods in determining the customs value of the compensating products in accordance with Article 32 (1) (b) (i) or, if the value cannot be determined in that way, the difference between the customs value of the compensating products and the processing costs determined by reasonable means.

▼B

However,
- certain charges determined in accordance with the committee procedure shall not be taken into account in calculating the amount to be deducted;
- where, prior to being placed under the outward processing procedure, the temporary export goods were released for free circulation at a reduced rate by virtue of their end use, and for as long as the conditions for granting the reduced rate continue to apply, the amount to be deducted shall be the amount of import duties actually levied when the goods were released for free circulation.
3. Where temporary export goods could qualify on their release for free circulation for a

reduced or zero rate of duty by virtue of their end use, that rate shall be taken into account provided that the goods underwent operations consistent with such an end-use in the country where the processing operation or last such operation took place.

4. Where compensating products qualify for a preferential tariff measure within the meaning of Article 20 (3) (d) or (e) and the measure exists for goods falling within the same tariff classification as the temporary export goods, the rate of import duty to be taken into account in establishing the amount to be deducted pursuant to paragraph 1 shall be that which would apply if the temporary export goods fulfilled the conditions under which that preferential measure may be applied.

5. This Article shall be without prejudice to the application of provisions, adopted or liable to be adopted in the context of trade between the Community and third countries, which provide for relief from import duties in respect of certain compensating products.

Article 152

1. Where the purpose of the processing operation is the repair of the temporary export goods, they shall be released for free circulation with total relief from import duties where it is established to the satisfaction of the customs authorities that the goods were repaired free of charge, either because of a contractual or statutory obligation arising from a guarantee or because of a manufacturing defect.

2. Paragraph 1 shall not apply where account was taken of the defect at the time when the goods in question were first released for free circulation.

Article 153

Where the purpose of the processing operation is the repair of temporary export goods and such repair is carried out in return for payment, the partial relief from import duties provided for in Article 145 shall be granted by establishing the amount of the duties applicable on the basis of the taxation elements pertaining to the compensating products on the date of acceptance of the declaration of release for free circulation of those products and taking into account as the customs value an amount equal to the repair costs, provided that those costs represent the only consideration provided by the holder of the authorization and are not influenced by any links between that holder and the operator.

▼M3

By way of derogation from Article 151, the committee procedure may be used to determine the cases in and specific conditions under which goods may be released for free circulation following an outwardprocessing operation, with the cost of the processing operation being taken as the basis for assessment for the purpose of applying the Customs Tariff of the European Communities.

▼B

IV. Outward-processing with use of the standard exchange system

Article 154

1. Under the conditions laid down in this Section IV which are applicable in addition to the preceding provisions, the standard exchange system shall permit an imported product, hereinafter referred to as a 'replacement product', to replace a compensating product.
2. The customs authorities shall allow the standard exchange system to be used where the processing operation involves the repair of Community goods other than those subject to the common agricultural policy or to the specific arrangements applicable to certain goods resulting from the processing of agricultural products.
3. Without prejudice to Article 159, the provisions applicable to compensating products shall also apply to replacement products.
4. The customs authorities shall, under the conditions they lay down, permit replacement products to be imported before the temporary export goods are exported (prior importation). In the event of prior importation of a replacement, security shall be provided to cover the amount of the import duties.

Article 155

1. Replacement products shall have the same tariff classification, be of the same commercial quality and possess the same technical characteristics as the temporary export goods had the latter undergone the repair in question.
2. Where the temporary export goods have been used before export, the replacement products must also have been used and may not be new products. The customs

authorities may, however, grant derogations from this rule if the replacement product has been supplied free of charge either because of a contractual or statutory obligation arising from a guarantee or because of a manufacturing defect.

Article 156

Standard exchange shall be authorized only where it is possible to verify that the conditions laid down in Article 155 are fulfilled.

Article 157

1. In the case of prior importation, the export goods shall be temporarily exported within a period of two months from the date of acceptance by the customs authorities of the declaration relating to the release of the replacement products for free circulation.
2. However, where exceptional circumstances so warrant, the customs authorities may, at the request of the person concerned, extend within reasonable limits the period referred to in paragraph 1.

Article 158

In the case of prior importation and where Article 151 is applied, the amount to be deducted shall be determined on the basis of the items of charge applicable to the temporary export goods on the date of acceptance of the declaration placing them under the procedure.

▼B

Article 159

Article 147 (2) and Article 148 (b) shall not apply in the context of standard exchange.

V. Other provision

Article 160

The procedures provided for within the framework of out-ward processing shall also be applicable for the purposes of implementing non-tariff common commercial policy measures.

Section 4
Export

Article 161

1. The export procedure shall allow Community goods to leave the customs territory of the Community. Exportation shall entail the application of exit formalities including commercial policy measures and, where appropriate, export duties.
2. With the exception of goods placed under the out-ward processing procedure or a transit procedure pursuant to Article 163, and without prejudice to Article 164, all Community goods intended for export shall be placed under the export procedure.
3. Goods dispatched to Helgoland shall not be considered to be exports from the customs territory of the Community.
4. The case in which and the conditions under which goods leaving the customs territory of the Community are not subject to an export declaration shall be determined in accordance with the committee procedure.
5. The export declaration must be lodged at the customs office responsible for supervising the place where the exporter is established or where the goods are packed or loaded for export shipment. Derogations shall be determined in accordance with the committee procedure.

Article 162

Release for export shall be granted on condition that the goods in question leave the customs territory of the Community in the same condition as when the export declaration was accepted.

Section 5
Internal transit

Article 163

1. The internal transit procedure shall, under the conditions laid down in paragraphs 2 to 4, allow the movement of Community goods from one point to another within the customs

territory of the Community passing through the territory of a third country without any change in their customs status. This provision shall be without prejudice to the application of Article 91 (1) (b).

2. The movement referred to in paragraph 1 may take place either:

▼B

(a) under the internal Community transit procedure, provided that such a possibility is provided for in an international agreement;

(b) under cover of a TIR carnet (TIR Convention);

(c) under cover of an ATA carnet ?M1 _____ ? used as a transit document;

(d) under cover of a Rhine Manifest (Article 9 of the Revised Convention for the Navigation of the Rhine);

(e) under cover of form 302 as provided for in the agreement between the States party to the North Atlantic Treaty on the status of their forces, signed in London on 19 June 1951, or

(f) by post (including parcel post).

3. In the case referred to in paragraph 2 (a), Articles 92, 94, 95, 96 and 97 shall apply mutatis mutandis.

4. In the cases referred to in paragraph 2 (b) to (f) goods shall keep their customs status only if that status is established under the conditions and in the form prescribed by the provisions adopted in accordance with the committee procedure.

Article 164

The conditions under which Community goods may move, without being subject to a customs procedure, from one point to another within the customs territory of the Community and temporarily out of that territory without alteration of their customs status shall be determined in accordance with the committee procedure.

Article 165

The internal Community transit procedure shall also apply where a Community provision makes express provision for its application.

CHAPTER 3
OTHER TYPES OF CUSTOMS-APPROVED TREATMENT OR USE

Section 1
Free zones and free warehouses

A. General

Article 166

Free zones and free warehouses shall be parts of the customs territory of the Community or premises situated in that territory and separated from the rest of it in which:
(a) Community goods are considered, for the purpose of import duties and commercial policy import measures, as not being on Community customs territory, provided they are not released for free circulation or placed under another customs procedure or used or consumed under conditions other than those provided for in customs regulations;
(b) Community goods for which such provision is made under Community legislation governing specific fields qualify, by virtue of being placed in a free zone or free warehouse, for measures normally attaching to the export of goods.

▼B

Article 167

1. Member States may designate parts of the customs territory of the Community as free zones or authorize the establishment of free warehouses.
2. Member States shall determine the area covered by each zone. Premises which are to be designated as free warehouses must be approved by Member States.

▼M3

3. Free zones with the exception of those designated in accordance with Article 168a, shall be enclosed. The Member States shall define the entry and exit points of each free zone or free warehouse.

▼B

4. The construction of any building in a free zone shall require the prior approval of the

customs authorities.

Article 168

▼M3

1. The perimeter and the entry and exit points of free zones, except the free zones designated in accordance with Article 168a, and of free warehouses shall be subject to supervision by the customs authorities.

▼B

2. Persons and means of transport entering or leaving a free zone or free warehouse may be subjected to a customs check.
3. Access to a free zone or free warehouse may be denied to persons who do not provide every guarantee necessary for compliance with the rules provided for in this Code.
4. The customs authorities may check goods entering, leaving or remaining in a free zone or free warehouse. To enable such checks to be carried out, a copy of the transport document, which shall accompany goods entering or leaving, shall be handed to, or kept at the disposal of, the customs authority by any person designated for this purpose by such authorities. Where such checks are required, the goods shall be made available to the customs authorities.

▼M3

Article 168a

1. The customs authorities may designate free zones in which customs checks and formalities shall be carried out and the provisions concerning customs debt applied in accordance with the requirements of the customs warehousing procedure. Articles 170, 176 and 180 shall not apply to the free zones thus designated.
2. References to free zones in Articles 37, 38 and 205 shall not apply to free zones referred to in paragraph 1.B. Placing of goods in free zones or free warehouses

▼B

Article 169

Both Community and non-Community goods may be placed in a free zone or free warehouse. However, the customs authorities may require that goods which present a danger or are likely to spoil other goods or which, for other reasons, require special facilities be placed in premises specially equipped to receive them.

▼B

Article 170

1. Without prejudice to Article 168 (4), goods entering a free zone or free warehouse need not be presented to the customs authorities, nor need a customs declaration be lodged.

▼M4

2. Goods shall be presented to the customs authorities and undergo the prescribed customs formalities where:
   (a) they have been placed under a customs procedure which is discharged when they enter a free zone or free warehouse; however, where the customs procedure in question permits exemption from the obligation to present goods, such presentation shall not be required;
   (b) they have been placed in a free zone or free warehouse on the basis of a decision to grant repayment or remission of import duties;
   (c) they qualify for the measures referred to in Article 166(b);
   (d) they enter a free zone or free warehouse directly from outside the customs territory of the Community.

▼B

3. Customs authorities may require goods subject to export duties or to other export provisions to be notified to the customs department.
4. At the request of the party concerned, the customs authorities shall certify the Community or non-Community status of goods placed in a free zone or free warehouse.

C. Operation of free zones and free warehouses

Article 171

1. There shall be no limit to the length of time goods may remain in free zones or free warehouses.

2. For certain goods referred to in Article 166 (b) which are covered by the common agricultural policy, specific time limits may be imposed in accordance with the committee procedure.

Article 172

1. Any industrial, commercial or service activity shall, under the conditions laid down in this Code, be authorized in a free zone or free warehouse. The carrying on of such activities shall be notified in advance to the customs authorities.
2. The customs authorities may impose certain prohibitions or restrictions on the activities referred to in paragraph 1, having regard to the nature of the goods concerned or the requirements of customs supervision.
3. The customs authorities may prohibit persons who do not provide the necessary guarantees of compliance with the provisions laid down in this Code from carrying on an activity in a free zone or free warehouse.

Article 173

Non-Community goods placed in a free zone or free warehouse may, while they remain in a free zone or free warehouse:

(a) be released for free circulation under the conditions laid down by that procedure and by Article 178;

(b) undergo the usual forms of handling referred to in Article 109 (1) without authorization;

▼B

(c) be placed under the inward processing procedure under the conditions laid down by that procedure. However, processing operations within the territory of the old free port of Hamburg, in the free zones of the Canary Islands, Azores, Madeira and overseas departments shall not be subject to economic conditions. However, with regard to the old free port of Hamburg, if conditions of competition in a specific economic sector in the Community are affected as a result of this derogation, the Council, acting by a qualified majority on a proposal from the Commission, shall decide that economic conditions shall apply to the corresponding economic activity within the territory of the old free port of Hamburg;

(d) be placed under the procedure for processing under customs control under the conditions laid down by that procedure;
(e) be placed under the temporary importation procedure under the conditions laid down by that procedure;
(f) be abandoned in accordance with Article 182;
(g) be destroyed, provided that the person concerned supplies the customs authorities with all the information they judge necessary. Where goods are placed under one of the procedures referred to in (c),
(d) or (e), the Member States may, in so far as is necessary to take account of the operating and customs supervision conditions of the free zones or free warehouses, adapt the control arrangements laid down.

Article 174

The Community goods referred to in Article 166 (b) which are covered by the common agricultural policy shall under-go only the forms of handling expressly prescribed for such goods in conformity with Article 109 (2). Such handling may be undertaken without authorization.

Article 175

1. Where Articles 173 and 174 are not applied, non-Community goods and the Community goods referred to in Article 166 (b) shall not be consumed or used in free zones or in free warehouses.
2. Without prejudice to the provisions applicable to supplies or stores, where the procedure concerned so provides, paragraph 1 shall not preclude the use or consumption of goods the release for free circulation or temporary importation of which would not entail application of import duties or measures under the common agricultural policy or commercial policy. In that event, no declaration of release for free circulation or temporary importation shall be required. Such declaration shall, however, be required if such goods are to be charged against a quota or a ceiling.

Article 176

1. All persons carrying on an activity involving the storage, working or processing, or sale

or purchase, of goods in a free zone or free warehouse shall keep stock records in a form approved by the customs authorities. Goods shall be entered in the stock records as soon as they are brought into the premises of such person. The stock records must enable the customs authorities to identify the goods, and must record their movements.

▼B

2. Where goods are transhipped within a free zone, the records relating to the operation shall be kept at the disposal of the customs authorities. The short-term storage of goods in connection with such transhipment shall be considered to be an integral part of the operation. For goods brought into a free zone directly from outside the customs territory of the Community or out of a free zone directly leaving the customs territory of the Community, a summary declaration shall be lodged in accordance with Articles 36a to 36c or 182a to 182d, as appropriate.

▼B

D. Removal of goods from free zones or free warehouses

Article 177

Without prejudice to special provisions adopted under customs legislation governing specific fields, goods leaving a free zone or free warehouse may be:
- exported or re-exported from the customs territory of the Community, or
- brought into another part of the customs territory of the Community. The provisions of Title III, with the exception of Articles 48 to 53 where Community goods are concerned, shall apply to goods brought into other parts of that territory except in the case of goods which leave that zone by sea or air without being placed under a transit or other customs procedure.

Article 178

1. Where a customs debt is incurred in respect of non-Community goods and the customs value of such goods is based on a price actually paid or payable which includes the cost of warehousing or of preserving goods while they remain in the free zone or free warehouse, such costs shall not be included in the customs value if they are shown

separately from the price actually paid or payable for the goods.
2. Where the said goods have undergone, in a free zone or free warehouse, one of the usual forms of handling within the meaning of Article 109 (1), the nature of the goods, the customs value and the quantity to be taken into consideration in determining the amount of import duties shall, at the request of the declarant and provided that such handling was covered by an authorization granted in accordance with paragraph 3 of that Article, be those which would be taken into account in respect of those goods, at the time referred to in Article 214, had they not undergone such handling. Derogations from this provision may, however, be determined in accordance with the committee procedure.

Article 179

1. Community goods referred to in Article 166 (b) which are covered by the common agricultural policy and are placed in a free zone or free warehouse shall be assigned a treatment or use provided for by the rules under which they are eligible, by virtue of their being placed in a free zone or free warehouse, for measures normally attaching to the export of such goods.
2. Should such goods be returned to another part of the customs territory of the Community, or if no application for their assignment to a treatment or use referred to in paragraph 1 has been made by the expiry of the period prescribed pursuant to Article 171 (2), the customs authorities shall take the measures laid down by the relevant legislation

▼M4

governing specific fields relating to failure to comply with the specified treatment or use.

Article 180

1. Where goods are brought into or returned to another part of the customs territory of the Community or placed under a customs procedure, the certificate referred to in Article 170 (4) may be used as proof of the Community or non-Community status of such goods.
2. Where it is not proved by the certificate or other means that the goods have Community

or non-Community status, the goods shall be considered to be:
- Community goods, for the purposes of applying export duties and export licences or export measures laid down under the commercial policy;
- non-Community goods in all other cases.

▼M4

Article 181

The customs authorities shall satisfy themselves that the rules governing exportation, outward processing, re-exportation, suspensive procedures or the internal transit procedure, as well as the provisions of Title V, are respected where goods are to leave the customs territory of the Community from a free zone or free warehouse.

▼B

Section 2
Re-exportation, destruction and abandonment

Article 182

1. Non-Community goods may be:
   - re-exported from the customs territory of the Community;
   - destroyed;
   - abandoned to the exchequer where national legislation makes provision to that effect.
2. Re-exportation shall, where appropriate, involve application of the formalities laid down for goods leaving, including commercial policy measures. Cases in which non-Community goods may be placed under a suspensive arrangement with a view to non-application of commercial policy measures on exportation may be determined in accordance with the committee procedure.
3. ►M1 Save in cases determined in accordance with the committee procedure, ?M4 _____ - destruction shall be the subject of prior notification of the customs authorities. - The customs authorities shall prohibit re-exportation should the formalities or measures referred to in the first subparagraph of paragraph 2 so provide. Where goods are placed under an economic customs procedure when on Community

customs territory are intended for re-exportation, a customs declaration within the meaning of Articles 59 to 78 shall be lodged. In such cases, Article 161 (4) and (5) shall apply. Abandonment shall be put into effect in accordance with national provisions.

4. Destruction or abandonment shall not entail any expense for the exchequer.

▼B

5. Any waste or scrap resulting from destruction shall be assigned a customs-approved treatment or use prescribed for non-Community goods. It shall remain under customs supervision until the time laid down in Article 37 (2).

TITLE V
GOODS LEAVING THE CUSTOMS TERRITORY OF THE COMMUNITY

▼M4

Article 182a

1. Goods leaving the customs territory of the Community, with the exception of goods carried on means of transport only passing through the territorial waters or the airspace of the customs territory without a stop within this territory, shall be covered either by a customs declaration or, where a customs declaration is not required, a summary declaration.

2. The committee procedure shall be used to establish:
   - the time limit by which the customs declaration or a summary declaration is to be lodged at the customs office of export before the goods are brought out of the customs territory of the Community,
   - the rules for exceptions from and variations to the time limit referred to above,
   - the conditions under which the requirement for a summary declaration may be waived or adapted, and
   - the cases in which and the conditions under which goods leaving the customs territory of the Community are not subject to either a customs declaration or a summary declaration, in accordance with the specific circumstances and for particular types of goods traffic, modes of transport and economic operators and where international

agreements provide for special security arrangements.

Article 182b

1. Where goods leaving the customs territory of the Community are assigned to a customs approved treatment or use for the purpose of which a customs declaration is required under the customs rules, this customs declaration shall be lodged at the customs office of export before the goods are to be brought out of the customs territory of the Community.
2. Where the customs office of export is different from the customs office of exit, the customs office of export shall immediately communicate or make available electronically the necessary particulars to the customs office of exit.
3. The customs declaration shall contain at least the particulars necessary for the summary declaration referred to in Article 182d(1).
4. Where the customs declaration is made other than by use of a data processing technique, the customs authorities shall apply the same level of risk management to the data as that applied to customs declarations made using a data processing technique.

Article 182c

1. Where goods leaving the customs territory of the Community are not assigned to a customs approved treatment or use for which a

▼B

customs declaration is required, a summary declaration shall be lodged at the customs office of exit before the goods are to be brought out of the customs territory of the Community.
2. Customs authorities may allow the summary declaration to be lodged at another customs office, provided that this office immediately communicates or makes available electronically the necessary particulars to the customs office of exit.
3. Customs authorities may accept, instead of the lodging of a summary declaration, the lodging of a notification and access to the summary declaration data in the economic operator's computer system.

Article 182d

1. The committee procedure shall be used to establish a common data set and format for the summary declaration, containing the particulars necessary for risk analysis and the proper application of customs controls, primarily for security and safety purposes, using, where appropriate, international standards and commercial practices.
2. The summary declaration shall be made using a data processing technique. Commercial, port or transport information may be used, provided that it contains the necessary particulars. Customs authorities may accept paper-based summary declarations in exceptional circumstances, provided that they apply the same level of risk management as that applied to summary declarations made using a data processing technique.
3. The summary declaration shall be lodged by:
   (a) the person who brings the goods, or who assumes responsibility for the carriage of the goods, out of the customs territory of the Community; or
   (b) any person who is able to present the goods in question or to have them presented to the competent customs authority; or
   (c) a representative of one of the persons referred to in points (a) or (b).
4. The person referred to in paragraph 3 shall, at his request, be authorised to amend one or more particulars of the summary declaration after it has been lodged. However, no amendment shall be possible after the customs authorities:
   (a) have informed the person who lodged the summary declaration that they intend to examine the goods; or
   (b) have established that the particulars in questions are incorrect; or
   (c) have allowed the removal of the goods.

▼B

Article 183

Goods leaving the customs territory of the Community shall be subject to customs supervision. They may be the subject of checks by the customs authorities in accordance with the provisions in force. They shall leave the said territory using, where appropriate, the route determined by the customs authorities and in accordance with the procedures laid down by those authorities.

▼M4

TITLE VI
PRIVILEGED OPERATIONS

CHAPTER 1
RELIEFS FROM CUSTOMS DUTY

Article 184

The Council shall, acting by a qualified majority on a proposal from the Commission, determine the cases in which, on account of special circumstances, relief from import duties or export duties shall be granted where goods are released for free circulation or exported.

CHAPTER 2
RETURNED GOODS

Article 185

1. Community goods which, having been exported from the customs territory of the Community, are returned to that territory and released for free circulation within a period of three years shall, at the request of the person concerned, be granted relief from import duties. However:
   - the three-year period may be exceeded in order to take account of special circumstances;
   - where, prior to their exportation from the customs territory of the Community, the returned goods had been released for free circulation at reduced or zero import duty because of their use for a particular purpose exemption from duty under paragraph 1 shall be granted only if they are to be re-imported for the same purpose. Where the purpose for which the goods in question are to be imported is no longer the same, the amount of import duties chargeable upon them shall be reduced by any amount levied on the goods when they were first released for free circulation. Should the latter amount exceed that levied on the entry for free circulation of returned goods, no refund shall be granted.

2. The relief from import duties provided for in paragraph 1 shall not be granted in the case of:
   (a) goods exported from the customs territory of the Community under the outward processing procedure unless those goods remain in the state in which they were exported;
   (b) goods which have been the subject of a Community measure involving their exportation to third countries. The circumstances in which and the conditions under which this requirement may be waived shall be determined in accordance with the procedure of the committee.

Article 186
The relief from import duties provided for in Article 185 shall be granted only if goods are reimported in the state in which they were exported. The circumstances in which and the conditions under which this requirement may be waived shall be determined in accordance with the procedure of the committee.
▼B

Article 187
Articles 185 and 186 shall apply mutatis mutandis to compensating products originally exported or re-exported subsequent to an inward processing procedure. The amount of import duty legally owed shall be determined on the basis of the rules applicable under the inward processing procedure, the date of re-export being regarded as the date of release for free circulation.

CHAPTER 3
PRODUCTS OF SEA-FISHING AND OTHER PRODUCTS TAKEN FROM THE SEA

Article 188
Without prejudice to Article 23 (1) (f), the following shall be exempt from import duties when they are released for free circulation:

(a) products of sea-fishing and other products taken from the territorial sea of a third country by vessels registered or recorded in a Member State and flying the flag of that state;

(b) products obtained from products referred to in (a) on board factoryships fulfilling the conditions laid down in that subparagraph.

TITLE VII
CUSTOMS DEBT

CHAPTER 1
SECURITY TO COVER CUSTOMS DEBT

Article 189

1. Where, in accordance with customs rules, the customs authorities requiresecurity to be provided in order to ensure payment of a customs debt, such security shall be provided by the person who is liable or who may become liable for that debt.
2. The customs authorities shall require only one security to be provided in respect of one customs debt. Where security is provided under a customs procedure which may be used for specific goods in several Member States, that security shall, as laid down in the provisions adopted under the committee procedure, be valid in the Member States concerned.
3. The customs authorities may authorize the security to be provided by a person other than the person from whom it is required.
4. Where the person who has incurred or who may incur a customs debt is a public authority, no security shall be required.
5. The customs authorities may waive the requirement for provision of security where the amount to be secured does not exceed ECU 500.

Article 190

1. Where customs legislation provides that the provision of security is optional, such

security shall be required at the discretion of the customs authorities in so far as they consider that a customs debt which has been or may be incurred is not certain to be paid within the prescribed period.

▼B

Where the security referred to in the preceding subparagraph is not required, the customs authorities may nevertheless require from the person referred to in Article 189 (1) an undertaking to comply with the obligations which that person is legally obliged to fulfil.

2. The security referred to in the first subparagraph of paragraph 1 shall be required:
   - at the time of application of the rules requiring such security to be provided, or
   - at any subsequent time when the customs authorities find that the customs debt which has been or may be incurred is not certain to be paid within the prescribed period.

Article 191

At the request of the person referred to in Article 189 (1) or (3), the customs authorities shall allow comprehensive security to be provided to cover two or more operations in respect of which a customs debt has been or may be incurred.

Article 192

▼M2

1. Where customs legislation makes it compulsory for security to be provided, and subject to the specific provisions laid down for transit in accordance with the committee procedure, the customs authorities shall fix the amount of such security at a level equal to:

▼B

- the precise amount of the customs debt or debts in question where that amount can be established with certainty at the time when the security is required,
- in other cases the maximum amount, as estimated by the customs authorities, of the customs debt or debts which have been or may be

incurred. Where comprehensive security is provided for customs debts which vary in amount over time, the amount of such security shall be set at a level enabling the customs debts in question to be covered at all times.

2. Where customs legislation provides that the provision of security is optional and the customs authorities require security to be provided, the amount of the security shall be fixed by those authorities so as not to exceed the level provided for in paragraph 1.

3. The circumstances in which and the conditions under which a flatrate security may be provided shall be determined in accordance with the procedure of the committee.

Article 193

Security may be provided by either:

- a cash deposit, or
- a guarantor.

Article 194

1. A cash deposit shall be made in the currency of the Member State in which the security is required. The following shall be deemed equivalent to a cash deposit:

▼B

- submission of a cheque the payment of which is guaranteed by the institution on which it is drawn in any manner acceptable to the customs authorities,
- submission of any other instrument recognized by those authorities as a means of payment.

2. Security in the form of a cash deposit or payment deemed equivalent to a cash deposit shall be given in accordance with the provisions in force in the Member State in which the security is required.

Article 195

The guarantor shall undertake in writing to pay jointly and severally with the debtor the secured amount of a customs debt which falls to be paid. The guarantor must be a third person established in the Community and approved by the customs authorities of the Member State. The customs authorities may refuse to approve the guarantor or type of security proposed where the latter do not appear certain to ensure payment of the customs debt within the prescribed period.

Article 196

The person required to provide security shall be free to choose between the types of security laid down in Article 193. However, the customs authorities may refuse to accept the type of security proposed where it is incompatible with the proper functioning of the customs procedure concerned. The same shall apply as regards the security proposed. The customs authorities may require that the type of security chosen be maintained for a specific period.

Article 197

1. Where the rules adopted in accordance with the committee procedure so provide, the customs authorities may accept types of security other than those referred to in Article 193 where they provide equivalent assurance that the customs debt will be paid. The customs authorities shall refuse the security proposed by the debtor where they do not consider that such security is certain to ensure payment of the customs debt.
2. Subject to the reservation referred to in the second subparagraph of paragraph 1, the customs authorities may accept a cash deposit without the conditions laid down in Article 194 (1) being fulfilled.

Article 198

Where the customs authorities establish that the security provided does not ensure, or is no longer certain or sufficient to ensure, payment of the customs debt within the prescribed period, they shall require the person referred to in Article 189 (1), at his option, to provide additional security or to replace the original security with a new security.

Article 199

1. The security shall not be released until such time as the customs debt in respect of which it was given is extinguished or can no longer arise. Once the customs debt is extinguished or can no longer arise, the security shall be released forthwith.

▼B

2. Once the customs debt has been extinguished in part or may arise only in respect of part of the amount which has been secured, part of the security shall be released accordingly at the request of the person concerned, unless the amount involved does not justify such

action.

Article 200

Provisions derogating from those contained in this chapter shall, where necessary, be adopted in accordance with committee procedure in order to take account of international conventions.

CHAPTER 2
INCURRENCE OF A CUSTOMS DEBT

Article 201

1. A customs debt on importation shall be incurred through:
   (a) the release for free circulation of goods liable to import duties, or
   (b) the placing of such goods under the temporary importation procedure with partial relief from import duties.
2. A customs debt shall be incurred at the time of acceptance of the customs declaration in question.
3. The debtor shall be the declarant. In the event of indirect representation, the person on whose behalf the customs declaration is made shall also be a debtor. Where a customs declaration in respect of one of the procedures referred to in paragraph 1 is drawn up on the basis of information which leads to all or part of the duties legally owed not being collected, the persons who provided the information required to draw up the declaration and who knew, or who ought reasonably to have known that such information was false, may also be considered debtors in accordance with the national provisions in force.

Article 202

1. A customs debt on importation shall be incurred through:
   (a) the unlawful introduction into the customs territory of the Community of goods liable to import duties, or
   (b) the unlawful introduction into another part of that territory of such goods located in a

free zone or free warehouse. For the purpose of this Article, unlawful introduction means any introduction in violation of the provisions of Articles 38 to 41 and the second indent of Article 177.
2. The customs debt shall be incurred at the moment when the goods are unlawfully introduced.
3. The debtors shall be:
   - the person who introduced such goods unlawfully,
   - any persons who participated in the unlawful introduction of the goods and who were aware or should reasonably have been aware that such introduction was unlawful, and
   - any persons who acquired or held the goods in question and who were aware or should reasonably have been aware at the time of acquiring or receiving the goods that they had been introduced unlawfully.

▼B

Article 203

1. A customs debt on importation shall be incurred through:
   - the unlawful removal from customs supervision of goods liable to import duties.
2. The customs debt shall be incurred at the moment when the goods are removed from customs supervision.
3. The debtors shall be:
   - the person who removed the goods from customs supervision,
   - any persons who participated in such removal and who were aware or should reasonably have been aware that the goods were being removed from customs supervision,
   - any persons who acquired or held the goods in question and who were aware or should reasonably have been aware at the time of acquiring or receiving the goods that they had been removed from customs supervision, and
   - where appropriate, the person required to fulfil the obligations arising from temporary storage of the goods or from the use of the customs procedure under which those goods are placed.

Article 204

1. A customs debt on importation shall be incurred through:
   (a) non-fulfilment of one of the obligations arising, in respect of goods liable to import duties, from their temporary storage or from the use of the customs procedure under which they are placed, or
   (b) non-compliance with a condition governing the placing of the goods under that procedure or the granting of a reduced or zero rate of import duty by virtue of the end-use of the goods, in cases other than those referred to in Article 203 unless it is established that those failures have no significant effect on the correct operation of the temporary storage or customs procedure in question.
2. The customs debt shall be incurred either at the moment when the obligation whose non-fulfilment gives rise to the customs debt ceases to be met or at the moment when the goods are placed under the customs procedure concerned where it is established subsequently that a condition governing the placing of the goods under the said procedure or the granting of a reduced or zero rate of import duty by virtue of the end-use of the goods was not in fact fulfilled.
3. The debtor shall be the person who is required, according to the circumstances, either to fulfil the obligations arising, in respect of goods liable to import duties, from their temporary storage or from the use of the customs procedure under which they have been placed, or to comply with the conditions governing the placing of the goods under that procedure.

Article 205

1. A customs debt on importation shall be incurred through:
   - the consumption or use, in a free zone or a free warehouse, of goods liable to import duties, under conditions other than those laid down by the legislation in force. Where goods disappear and where their disappearance cannot be explained to the satisfaction of the customs authorities, those authorities may regard the goods as having been consumed or used in the free zone or the free warehouse.

▼B

2. The debt shall be incurred at the moment when the goods are consumed or are first

used under conditions other than those laid down by the legislation in force.
3. The debtor shall be the person who consumed or used the goods and any persons who participated in such consumption or use and who were aware or should reasonably have been aware that the goods were being consumed or used under conditions other than those laid down by the legislation in force. Where customs authorities regard goods which have disappeared as having been consumed or used in the free zone or the free warehouse and it is not possible to apply the preceding paragraph, the person liable for payment of the customs debt shall be the last person known to these authorities to have been in possession of the goods.

Article 206

1. By way of derogation from Articles 202 and 204 (1) (a), no customs debt on Importation shall be deemed to be incurred in respect of specific goods where the person concerned proves that the non-fulfilment of the obligations which arise from:
   - the provisions of Articles 38 to 41 and the second indent of Article 177, or
   - keeping the goods in question in temporary storage, or
   - the use of the customs procedure under which the goods have been placed, results from the total destruction or irretrievable loss of the said goods as a result of the actual nature of the goods or unforeseeable circumstances or force majeure, or as a consequence of authorization by the customs authorities. For the purposes of this paragraph, goods shall be irretrievably lost when they are rendered unusable by any person.
2. Nor shall a customs debt on importation be deemed to be incurred in respect of goods released for free circulation at a reduced or zero rate of import duty by virtue of their end-use, where such goods are exported or re-exported with the permission of the customs authorities.

Article 207

Where, in accordance with Article 206 (1), no customs debt is deemed to be incurred in respect of goods released for free circulation at a reduced or zero rate of import duty on account of their end-use, any scrap or waste resulting from such destruction shall be deemed to be non-Community goods.

Article 208

Where in accordance with Article 203 or 204 a customs debt is incurred in respect of goods released for free circulation at a reduced rate of import duty on account of their end-use, the amount paid when the goods were released for free circulation shall be deducted from the amount of the customs debt. This provision shall apply mutatis mutandis where a customs debt is incurred in respect of scrap and waste resulting from the destruction of such goods.

Article 209

1. A customs debt on exportation shall be incurred through:

▼B

- the exportation from the customs territory of the Community, under cover of a customs declaration, of goods liable to export duties.

2. The customs debt shall be incurred at the time when such customs declaration is accepted.
3. The debtor shall be the declarant. In the event of indirect representation, the person on whose behalf the declaration is made shall also be a debtor.

Article 210

1. A customs debt on exportation shall be incurred through:
   - the removal from the customs territory of the Community of goods liable to export duties without a customs declaration.
2. The customs debt shall be incurred at the time when the said goods actually leave that territory.
3. The debtor shall be:
   - the person who removed the goods, and
   - any persons who participated in such removal and who were aware or should reasonably have been aware that a customs declaration had not been but should have been lodged.

Article 211

1. A customs debt on exportation shall be incurred through:
   - failure to comply with the conditions under which the goods were allowed to leave the customs territory of the Community with total or partial relief from export duties.
2. The debt shall be incurred at the time when the goods reach a destination other than that for which they were allowed to leave the customs territory of the Community with total or partial relief from export duties or, should the customs authorities be unable to determine that time, the expiry of the time limit set for the production of evidence that the conditions entitling the goods to such relief have been fulfilled.
3. The debtor shall be the declarant. In the event of indirect representation, the person on whose behalf the declaration is made shall also be a debtor.

Article 212

The customs debt referred to in Articles 201 to 205 and 209 to 211 shall be incurred even if it relates to goods subject to measures of prohibition or restriction on importation or exportation of any kind whatsoever. However, no customs debt shall be incurred on the unlawful introduction into the customs territory of the Community of counterfeit currency or of narcotic drugs and psychotropic substances which do not enter into the economic circuit strictly supervised by the competent authorities with a view to their use for medical and scientific purposes. For the purposes of criminal law as applicable to customs offences, the customs debt shall nevertheless be deemed to have been incurred where, under a Member State's criminal law, customs duties provide the basis for determining penalties, or the existence of a customs debt is grounds for taking criminal proceedings.

▼M3

Article 212a

Where customs legislation provides for favourable tariff treatment of goods by reason of their nature or end-use or for relief or total or

▼B

partial exemption from import or export duties pursuant to Articles 21, 82, 145 or 184 to 187, such favourable tariff treatment, relief or exemption shall also apply in cases where a customs debt is incurred pursuant to Articles 202 to 205, 210 or 211, on condition that the

behaviour of the person concerned involves neither fraudulent dealing nor obvious negligence and he produces evidence that the other conditions for the application of favourable treatment, relief or exemption have been satisfied.
▼B

Article 213
Where several persons are liable for payment of one customs debt, they shall be jointly and severally liable for such debt.

Article 214
1. Save as otherwise expressly provided by this Code and without prejudice to paragraph 2, the amount of the import duty or export duty applicable to goods shall be determined on the basis of the rules of assessment appropriate to those goods at the time when the customs debt in respect of them is incurred.
2. Where it is not possible to determine precisely when the customs debt is incurred, the time to be taken into account in determining the rules of assessment appropriate to the goods concerned shall be the time when the customs authorities conclude that the goods are in a situation in which a customs debt is incurred. However, where the information available to the customs authorities enables them to establish that the customs debt was incurred prior to the time when they reached that conclusion, the amount of the import duty or export duty payable on the goods in question shall be determined on the basis of the rules of assessment appropriate to the goods at the earliest time when existence of the customs debt arising from the situation may be established from the information available.
3. Compensatory interest shall be applied, in the circumstances and under the conditions to be defined in the provisions adopted under the committee procedure, in order to prevent the wrongful acquisition of a financial advantage through deferment of the date on which the customs debt was incurred or entered in the accounts.
▼M2

Article 215
1. A customs debt shall be incurred:

- at the place where the events from which it arises occur,
- if it is not possible to determine that place, at the place where the customs authorities conclude that the goods are in a situation in which a customs debt is incurred,
- if the goods have been entered for a customs procedure which has not been discharged, and the place cannot be determined pursuant to the first or second indent within a period of time determined, if appropriate, in accordance with the committee procedure, at the place where the goods were either placed under the procedure concerned or were introduced into the Community customs territory under that procedure.

2. Where the information available to the customs authorities enables them to establish that the customs debt was already incurred when the goods were in another place at an earlier date, the customs debt shall be deemed to have been incurred at the place which may be established as the location of the goods at the earliest time when existence of the customs debt may be established.

▼M3

3. The customs authorities referred to in Article 217(1) are those of the Member State where the customs debt is incurred or is deemed to have been incurred in accordance with this Article.

▼M3

4. If a customs authority finds that a customs debt has been incurred under Article 202 in another Member State and the amount of that debt is lower than EUR 5 000, the debt shall be deemed to have been incurred in the Member State where the finding was made.

▼B

Article 216

1. In so far as agreements concluded between the Community and certain third countries provide for the granting on importation into those countries of preferential tariff treatment for goods originating in the Community within the meaning of such agreements, on condition that, where they have been obtained under the inward processing procedure, non-Community goods incorporated in the said originating goods

are subject to payment of the import duties payable thereon, the validation of the documents necessary to enable such preferential tariff treatment to be obtained in third countries shall cause a customs debt on importation to be incurred.
2. The moment when such customs debt is incurred shall be deemed to be the moment when the customs authorities accept the export declaration relating to the goods in question.
3. The debtor shall be the declarant. In the event of indirect representation, the person on whose behalf the declaration is made shall also be a debtor.
4. The amount of the import duties corresponding to this customs debt shall be determined under the same conditions as in the case of a customs debt resulting from the acceptance, on the same date, of the declaration for release for free circulation of the goods concerned for the purpose of terminating the inward processing procedure.

CHAPTER 3
RECOVERY OF THE AMOUNT OF THE CUSTOMS DEBT

Section 1
Entry in the accounts and communication of the amount of duty to the debtor

Article 217
1. Each and every amount of import duty or export duty resulting from a customs debt, hereinafter called 'amount of duty', shall be calculated by the customs authorities as soon as they have the necessary particulars, and entered by those authorities in the accounting records or on any other equivalent medium (entry in the accounts). The first subparagraph shall not apply:
(a) where a provisional anti-dumping or countervailing duty has been introduced;
▼M1
(b) where the amount of duty legally due exceeds that determined on the basis of binding information;
▼B
(c) where the provisions adopted in accordance with the committee procedure waive the

requirement for the customs authorities to enter in the accounts amounts of duty below a given level.

▼M2

The customs authorities may discount amounts of duty which, under Article 221 (3), could not be communicated to the debtor after the end of the time allowed.

2. The Member States shall determine the practical procedures for the entry in the accounts of the amounts of duty. Those procedures may differ according to whether or not, in view of the circumstances in which the customs debt was incurred, the customs authorities are satisfied that the said amounts will be paid.

Article 218

1. Where a customs debt is incurred as a result of the acceptance of the declaration of goods for a customs procedure other than temporary importation with partial relief from import duties or any other act having the same legal effect as such acceptance the amount corresponding to such customs debt shall be entered in the accounts as soon as it has been calculated and, at the latest, on the second day following that on which the goods were released. However, provided that payment has been secured, the total amount of duty relating to all the goods released to one and the same person during a period fixed by the customs authorities, which may not exceed 31 days, may be covered by a single entry in the accounts at the end of the period. Such entry in the accounts shall take place within five days of the expiry of the period in question.

2. Where it is provided that goods may be released subject to meeting certain conditions laid down by Community legislation which govern either determination of the amount of the debt or its collection, entry in the accounts shall take place no later than two days following the day on which the amount of the debt or the obligation to pay the duties resulting from that debt is determined or fixed. However, where the customs debt relates to a provisional anti-dumping or countervailing duty, that duty shall be entered in the accounts no later than two months following publication in the Official Journal of the European Communities of the Regulation establishing a definitive antidumping or countervailing duty.

3. Where a customs debt is incurred under conditions other than those referred to in

paragraph 1, the relevant amount of duty shall be entered in the accounts within two days of the date on which the customs authorities are in a position to:
(a) calculate the amount of duty in question, and
(b) determine the debtor.

Article 219

1. The time limits for entry in the accounts laid down in Article 218 may be extended:
   (a) for reasons relating to the administrative organization of the Member States, and in particular where accounts are centralized, or
   (b) where special circumstances prevent the customs authorities from complying with the said time limits. Such extended time limit shall not exceed 14 days.
2. The time limits laid down in paragraph 1 shall not apply in unforeseeable circumstances or in cases of force majeure.

Article 220

1. Where the amount of duty resulting from a customs debt has not been entered in the accounts in accordance with Articles 218 and 219 or

▼B

has been entered in the accounts at a level lower than the amount legally owed, the amount of duty to be recovered or which remains to be recovered shall be entered in the accounts within two days of the date on which the customs authorities become aware of the situation and are in a position to calculate the amount legally owed and to determine the debtor (subsequent entry in the accounts). That time limit may be extended in accordance with Article 219.

2. Except in the cases referred to in the second and third subparagraphs of Article 217 (1), subsequent entry in the accounts shall not occur where: (a) the original decision not to enter duty in the accounts or to enter it in the accounts at a figure less than the amount of duty legally owed was taken on the basis of general provisions invalidated at a later date by a court decision;

▼M3

(b) the amount of duty legally owed was not entered in the accounts as a result of an error on the part of the customs authorities which could not reasonably have been detected by the person liable for payment, the latter for his part having acted in good faith and complied with all the provisions laid down by the legislation in force as regards the customs declaration. Where the preferential status of the goods is established on the basis of a system of administrative cooperation involving the authorities of a third country, the issue of a certificate by those authorities, should it prove to be incorrect, shall constitute an error which could not reasonably have been detected within the meaning of the first subparagraph. The issue of an incorrect certificate shall not, however, constitute an error where the certificate is based on an incorrect account of the facts provided by the exporter, except where, in particular, it is evident that the issuing authorities were aware or should have been aware that the goods did not satisfy the conditions laid down for entitlement to the preferential treatment. The person liable may plead good faith when he can demonstrate that, during the period of the trading operations concerned, he has taken due care to ensure that all the conditions for the preferential treatment have been fulfilled. The person liable may not, however, plead good faith if the European Commission has published a notice in the Official Journal of the European Communities, stating that there are grounds for doubt concerning the proper application of the preferential arrangements by the beneficiary country;

▼B
(c) the provisions adopted in accordance with the committee procedure exempt the customs authority from the subsequent entry in the accounts of amounts of duty less than a certain figure.

Article 221

1. As soon as it has been entered in the accounts, the amount of duty shall be communicated to the debtor in accordance with appropriate procedures.
2. Where the amount of duty payable has been entered, for guidance, in the customs declaration, the customs authorities may specify that it shall not be communicated in accordance with paragraph 1 unless the amount of duty indicated does not correspond to the amount determined by the authorities. Without prejudice to the application of the second subparagraph of Article 218 (1), where use is made of the possibility provided

for in the preceding subparagraph, release of the goods by the customs autho-
▼B
rities shall be equivalent to communication to the debtor of the amount of duty entered in the accounts.
▼M3
3. Communication to the debtor shall not take place after the expiry of a period of three years from the date on which the customs debt was incurred. This period shall be suspended from the time an appeal within the meaning of Article 243 is lodged, for the duration of the appeal proceedings.
4. Where the customs debt is the result of an act which, at the time it was committed, was liable to give rise to criminal court proceedings, the amount may, under the conditions set out in the provisions in force, be communicated to the debtor after the expiry of the three-year period referred to in paragraph 3.
▼B

Section 2
Time limit and procedures for payment of the amount of duty

Article 222

1. Amounts of duty communicated in accordance with Article 221 shall be paid by debtors within the following periods: (a) if the person is not entitled to any of the payment facilities laid down in Articles 224 to 229, payment shall be made within the period prescribed. Without prejudice to the second paragraph of Article 244, that period shall not exceed ten days following communication to the debtor of the amount of duty owed and, in the case of aggregation of entries in the accounts under the conditions laid down in the second subparagraph of Article 218 (1), it shall be so fixed as not to enable the debtor to obtain a longer period for payment than if he had been granted deferred payment. An extension shall be granted automatically where it is established that the person concerned received the communication too late to enable him to make payment within the period prescribed. Extension of the period may also be granted by the customs authorities at the request of the debtor where the amount of duty to be paid

results from action for post-clearance recovery. Without prejudice to Article 229 (a), such extensions shall not exceed the time necessary for the debtor to take the appropriate steps to discharge his obligation; (b) if the person is entitled to any of the payment facilities laid down in Articles 224 to 229, payment shall be made no later than the expiry of the period or periods specified in relation to those facilities.

▼M3

2. The cases and conditions in which the debtor's obligation to pay duty shall be suspended may also be provided for in accordance with the committee procedure:
   - where an application for remission of duty is made in accordance with Article 236, 238 or 239, or
   - where goods are seized with a view to subsequent confiscation in accordance with the second indent of point (c) or with point (d) of Article 233, or
   - where the customs debt was incurred under Article 203 and there is more than one debtor.

▼B

Article 223

Payment shall be made in cash or by any other means with similar discharging effect in accordance with the provisions in force. It may also be made by adjustment of credit balance where the provisions in force so allow.

Article 224

Provided the amount of duty payable by the person concerned relates to goods declared for a customs procedure which entails the obligation to pay such duty, the customs authorities shall, at that person's request, grant deferment of payment of that amount under the conditions laid down in Articles 225, 226 and 227.

Article 225

The granting of deferment of payment shall be conditional on the provision of security by the applicant. In addition, the granting of deferment of payment may give rise to the charging of incidental expenses for the opening of files or for services rendered.

Article 226

The customs authorities shall decide which of the following procedures must be used when granting deferment of payment:

(a) separately in respect of each amount of duty entered in the accounts under the conditions laid down in the first subparagraph of Article 218 (1) or in Article 220 (1);

or

(b) globally in respect of all amounts of duty entered in the accounts under the conditions laid down in the first subparagraph of Article 218 (1) during a period fixed by the customs authorities not exceeding 31 days; or

(c) globally in respect of all amounts of duty forming a single entry in accordance with the second subparagraph of Article 218 (1).

Article 227

1. The period for which payment is deferred shall be 30 days. It shall be calculated as, follows:

   (a) where payment is deferred in accordance with Article 226 (a), the period shall be calculated from the day following the date on which the amount of duty is entered in the accounts by the customs authorities. Where Article 219 is applied, the period of 30 days calculated in accordance with the first subparagraph shall be reduced by the number of days corresponding to the period in excess of two days used to enter the amount in the accounts;

   (b) where payment is deferred in accordance with Article 226 (b), the period shall be calculated from the day following the date on which the aggregation period expires. It shall be reduced by the number of days corresponding to half the number of days in the aggregation period;

   (c) where payment is deferred in accordance with Article 226 (c), the period shall be calculated from the day following the expiry date of the period during which the goods in question were released. It shall

▼B

be reduced by the number of days corresponding to half the number of days in the period concerned.

2. Where the number of days in the periods referred to in paragraph 1 (b) and (c) is an odd number, the number of days to be deducted from the 30-day period pursuant to paragraph 1 (b) and (c) shall be equal to half the next lowest even number.
3. To simplify matters, where the periods referred to in paragraph 1 (b) and (c) are a calendar week or a calendar month, Member States may provide that the amount of duty in respect of which payment has been deferred shall be paid:
   (a) if the period is a calendar week, on the Friday of the fourth week following that calendar week;
   (b) if the period is a calendar month, by the sixteenth day of the month following that calendar month.

Article 228

1. Deferment of payment shall not be granted in respect of amounts of duty which, although relating to goods entered for a customs procedure which entails the obligation to pay such duty, are entered in the accounts in accordance with the provisions in force concerning acceptance of incomplete declarations, because the declarant has not, by the time of expiry of the period set, provided the information necessary for the definitive valuation of the goods for customs purposes or has not supplied the particulars or the document missing when the incomplete declaration was accepted.
2. However, deferment of payment may be granted in the cases referred to in paragraph 1 where the amount of duty to be recovered is entered in the accounts before the expiry of a period of 30 days from the date on which the amount originally charged was entered in the accounts or, if it was not entered in the accounts, from the date on which the declaration relating to the goods in question was accepted. The duration of the deferment of payment granted in such circumstances shall not extend beyond the date of expiry of the period which, pursuant to Article 227, was granted in respect of the amount of duty originally fixed, or which would have been granted had the amount of duty legally due been entered in the accounts when the goods in question were declared.

Article 229

The customs authorities may grant the debtor payment facilities other than deferred payment. The granting of such payment facilities shall:
(a) be conditional on the provision of security. However, such security need not be required where to require it would, because of the situation of the debtor, create serious economic or social difficulties;
(b) result in credit interest being charged over and above the amount of duty. The amount of such interest shall be calculated in such a way that it is equivalent to the amount which would be charged for this purpose on the national money or financial market of the currency in which the amount is payable. The customs authorities may refrain from claiming credit interest where to claim it would, because of the situation of the debtor, create serious economic or social difficulties.

▼B

Article 230

Whatever the payment facilities granted to the debtor, the latter may in any case pay all or part of the amount of duty without awaiting expiry of the period he has been granted for payment.

Article 231

An amount of duty owed may be paid by a third person instead of the debtor.

Article 232

1. Where the amount of duty due has not been paid within the prescribed period:
   (a) the customs authorities shall avail themselves of all options open to them under the legislation in force, including enforcement, to secure payment of that amount. Special provisions may be adopted, in accordance with committee procedure, in respect of guarantors within the framework of the transit procedure;
   (b) interest on arrears shall be charged over and above the amount of duty. The rate of interest on arrears may be higher than the rate of credit interest. It may not be lower than that rate.
2. The customs authorities may waive collection of interest on

arrears:
   (a) where, because of the situation of the debtor, it would be likely to create serious economic or social difficulties;
   (b) where the amount does not exceed a level fixed in accordance with the committee procedure, or
   (c) if the duty is paid within five days of the expiry of the period prescribed for payment.
3. The customs authorities may fix:
   (a) minimum periods for calculation of interest;
   (b) minimum amounts payable as interest on arrears.

CHAPTER 4
EXTINCTION OF CUSTOMS DEBT

Article 233

Without prejudice to the provisions in force relating to the time-barring of a customs debt and non-recovery of such a debt in the event of the legally established insolvency of the debtor, a customs debt shall be extinguished:
(a) by payment of the amount of duty;
(b) by remission of the amount of duty;
(c) where, in respect of goods declared for a customs procedure entailing the obligation to pay duties:
   - the customs declaration is invalidated -M1 _____ -,
   - the goods, before their release, are either seized and simultaneously or subsequently confiscated, destroyed on the instructions of the customs authorities, destroyed or abandoned in accordance with Article 182, or destroyed or irretrievably lost
▼B
as a result of their actual nature or of unforeseeable circumstances or force majeure;
(d) where goods in respect of which a customs debt is incurred in accordance with Article 202 are seized upon their unlawful introduction and are simultaneously or subsequently confiscated. In the event of seizure and confiscation, the customs debt shall, nonetheless for the purposes of the criminal law applicable to customs offences,

be deemed not to have been extinguished where, under a Member State's criminal law, customs duties provide the basis for determining penalties or the existence of a customs debt is grounds for taking criminal proceedings.

Article 234

A customs debt, as referred to in Article 216, shall also be extinguished where the formalities carried out in order to enable the preferential tariff treatment referred to in Article 216 to be granted are cancelled.

CHAPTER 5
REPAYMENT AND REMISSION OF DUTY

Article 235

The following definitions shall apply:
(a) 'repayment' means the total or partial refund of import duties or export duties which have been paid;
(b) 'remission' means either a decision to waive all or part of the amount of a customs debt or a decision to render void an entry in the accounts of all or part of an amount of import or export duty which has not been paid.

Article 236

1. Import duties or export duties shall be repaid in so far as it is established that when they were paid the amount of such duties was not legally owed or that the amount has been entered in the accounts contrary to Article 220 (2). Import duties or export duties shall be remitted in so far as it is established that when they were entered in the accounts the amount of such duties was not legally owed or that the amount has been entered in the accounts contrary to Article 220 (2). No repayment or remission shall be granted when the facts which led to the payment or entry in the accounts of an amount which was not legally owed are the result of deliberate action by the person concerned.

2. Import duties or export duties shall be repaid or remitted upon submission of an application to the appropriate customs office within a period of three years from the

date on which the amount of those duties was communicated to the debtor. That period shall be extended if the person concerned provides evidence that he was prevented from submitting his application within the said period as a result of unforeseeable circumstances or force majeure. Where the customs authorities themselves discover within this period that one or other of the situations described in the first and second subparagraphs of paragraph 1 exists, they shall repay or remit on their own initiative.

▼B

Article 237

Import duties or export duties shall be repaid where a customs declaration is invalidated and the duties have been paid. Repayment shall he granted upon submission of an application by the person concerned within the periods laid down for submission of the application for invalidation of the customs declaration.

Article 238

1. Import duties shall be repaid or remitted in so far as it is established that the amount of such duties entered in the accounts relates to goods placed under the customs procedure in question and rejected by the importer because at the point in time referred to in Article 67 they are defective or do not comply with the terms of the contract on the basis of which they were imported. Defective goods, within the meaning of the first subparagraph, shall be deemed to include goods damaged before their release.
2. Repayment or remission of import duties shall be granted on condition that:
    (a) the goods have not been used, except for such initial use as may have been necessary to establish that they were defective or did not comply with the terms of the contract;
    (h) the goods are exported from the customs territory of the Community. At the request of the person concerned, the customs authorities shall permit the goods to be destroyed ?C1 or to be placed, with a view to re-export, under the ? external transit procedure or the customs warehousing procedure or in a free zone or free warehouse, instead of being exported. For the purposes of being assigned one of the customs-approved treatments or uses provided for in the preceding subparagraph, the goods shall be deemed to be non-Community goods.

3. Import duties shall not be repaid or remitted in respect of goods which, before being declared to customs declaration, were imported temporarily for testing, unless it is established that the fact that the goods were defective or did not comply with the terms of the contract could not normally have been detected in the course of such tests.
4. Import duties shall be repaid or remitted for the reasons set out in paragraph 1 upon submission of an application to the appropriate customs office within twelve months from the date on which the amount of those duties was communicated to the debtor. However, the customs authorities may permit this period to be exceeded in duly justified exceptional cases.

Article 239

1. Import duties or export duties may be repaid or remitted in situations other than those referred to in Articles 236, 237 and 238:
   - to be determined in accordance with the procedure of the committee;
   - resulting from circumstances in which no deception or obvious negligence may be attributed to the person concerned. The situations in which this provision may be applied and the procedures to be followed to that end shall be defined in accordance with the committee procedure. Repayment or remission may be made subject to special conditions.

▼B
2. Duties shall be repaid or remitted for the reasons set out in paragraph 1 upon submission of an application to the appropriate customs office within 12 months from the date on which the amount of the duties was communicated to the debtor. However, the customs authorities may permit this period to be exceeded in duly justified exceptional cases.

Article 240

Import or export duties shall be repaid or remitted under the conditions laid down in this chapter only if the amount to be repaid or remitted exceeds an amount fixed in accordance with the procedure of the committee. However, the customs authorities may also grant an application for repayment or remission in respect of a lower amount.

Article 241

Repayment by the competent authorities of amounts of import duties or export duties or of credit interest or interest on arrears collected on payment of such duties shall not give rise to the payment of interest by those authorities. However, interest shall be paid:
- where a decision to grant a request for repayment is not implemented within three months of the date of adoption of that decision,
- where national provisions so stipulate. The amount of such interest shall be calculated in such a way that it is equivalent to the amount which would be charged for this purpose on the national money or financial market.

Article 242

Where a customs debt has been remitted or the corresponding amount of duty repaid in error, the original debt shall again become payable. Any interest paid under Article 241 must be reimbursed.

TITLE VIII
APPEALS

Article 243

1. Any person shall have the right to appeal against decisions taken by the customs authorities which relate to the application of customs legislation, and which concern him directly and individually. Any person who has applied to the customs authorities for a decision relating to the application of customs legislation and has not obtained a ruling on that request within the period referred to in Article 6 (2) shall also be entitled to exercise the right of appeal. The appeal must be lodged in the Member State where the decision has been taken or applied for.
2. The right of appeal may be exercised:
   (a) initially, before the customs authorities designated for that purpose by the Member States;
   (b) subsequently, before an independent body, which may be a judicial authority or an

equivalent specialized body, according to the provisions in force in the Member States.

▼B

Article 244

The lodging of an appeal shall not cause implementation of the disputed decision to be suspended. The customs authorities shall, however, suspend implementation of such decision in whole or in part where they have good reason to believe that the disputed decision is inconsistent with customs legislation or that irreparable damage is to be feared for the person concerned. Where the disputed decision has the effect of causing import duties or export duties to be charged, suspension of implementation of that decision shall be subject to the existence or lodging of a security. However, such security need not be required where such a requirement would be likely, owing to the debtor's circumstances, to cause serious economic or social difficulties.

Article 245

The provisions for the implementation of the appeals procedure shall be determined by the Member States.

Article 246

This title shall not apply to appeals lodged with a view to the annulment or revision of a decision taken by the customs authorities on the basis of criminal law.

TITLE IX
FINAL PROVISIONS

CHAPTER 1
CUSTOMS CODE COMMITTEE

▼M3

Article 247

The measures necessary for the implementation of this Regulation, including implementation of the Regulation referred to in Article 184, except for Title VIII and subject to Articles 9 and 10 of Regulation (EEC) No 2658/87 (1) and to Article 248 of this Regulation shall be adopted in accordance with the regulatory procedure referred to in Article 247a(2) in compliance with the international commitments entered into by the Community.

Article 247a

1. The Commission shall be assisted by a Customs Code Committee (hereinafter referred to as 'the Committee').
2. Where reference is made to this paragraph, Articles 5 and 7 of Decision 1999/468/EC shall apply, having regard to the provisions of Article 8 thereof.
   The period laid down in Article 5(6) of Decision 1999/468/EC shall be set at three months.
3. The Committee shall adopt its rules of procedure.

▼B

(1) OJ L 256, 7.9.1987, p. 1.

Article 248

The measures necessary for implementing Articles 11, 12 and 21 shall be adopted in accordance with the management procedure referred to in Article 248a(2).

Article 248a

1. The Commission shall be assisted by a Customs Code Committee, hereinafter referred to as 'the Committee'.
2. Where reference is made to this paragraph, Articles 4 and 7 of Decision 1999/468/EC shall apply. The period laid down in Article 4(3) of Decision 1999/468/EC shall be set at three months.
3. The Committee shall adopt its rules of procedure.

Article 249

The Committee may examine any question concerning customs legislation which is raised by its chairman, either on his own initiative or at the request of a Member State's representative.

▼B

CHAPTER 2
LEGAL EFFECTS IN A MEMBER STATE OF MEASURES TAKEN, DOCUMENTS ISSUED AND FINDINGS MADE IN ANOTHER MEMBER STATE

Article 250

Where a customs procedure is used in several Member States,
- the decisions, identification measures taken or agreed on, and the documents issued by the customs authorities of one Member State shall have the same legal effects in other Member States as such decisions, measures taken and documents issued by the customs authorities of each of those Member States;
- the findings made at the time controls are carried out by the customs authorities of a Member State shall have the same conclusive force in the other Member States as the findings made by the customs authorities of each of those Member States.

CHAPTER 3
OTHER FINAL PROVISIONS

Article 251

1. The following Regulations and Directives are hereby repealed:
   - Council Regulation (EEC) No 802/68 of 27 June 1968 on the common definition of the concept of the origin of goods (1)[74], as last amended by Regulation (EEC) No 456/91 (2)[75];
   - Council Regulation (EEC) No 754/76 of 25 March 1976 on the customs treatment applicable to goods returned to the customs territory of the Community (3)[76], as last amended by Regulation (EEC) No 1147/86 (4)[77];

▼M3
   - Council Regulation (EEC) No 2779/78 of 23 November 1978 on the procedure for applying the European unit of account (EUA) to legal acts adopted in the customs sphere (1)[78], as amended by Regulation (EEC) No 289/84 (2)[79];
   - Council Regulation (EEC) No 1430/79 of 2 July 1979 on the repayment or remission of import or export duties (3)[80], as last amended by Regulation (EEC) No 1854/89 (4)[81];
   - Council Regulation (EEC) No 1697/79 of 24 July 1979 on the postclearance recovery of import duties or export duties which have not been required of the person liable for payment on goods entered for a customs procedure involving the obligation to pay such duties (5)[82], as last amended by Regulation (EEC) No 1854/89 (6)[83];
   - Council Directive 79/695/EEC of 24 July 1979 on the harmonization of procedures for

---

74) OJ No L 148, 28.6.1968, p. 1.
75) OJ No L 54, 28.2.1991, p. 4.
76) OJ No L 89, 2.4.1976, p. 1.
77) OJ No L 105, 22.4.1986, p. 1.
78) OJ No L 333, 30.11.1978, p. 5.
79) OJ No L 33, 4.2.1984, p. 2.
80) OJ No L 175, 12.7.1979, p. 1.
81) OJ No L 186, 30.6.1989, p. 1.
82) OJ No L 197, 3.8.1979, p. 1.
83) OJ No L 186, 30.6.1989, p. 1.

the release of goods for free circulation (7)[84], as last amended by Directive 90/504/EEC (8)[85];
- Council Regulation (EEC) No 1224/80 of 28 May 1980 on the valuation of goods for customs purposes (9)[86], as last amended by the Regulation (EEC) No 4046/89 (10)[87];
- Council Directive 81/177/EEC of 24 February 1981 on the harmonization of procedures for the export of Community goods (11)[88], as last amended by Regulation (EEC) No 1854/89 (12)[89];
- Council Regulation (EEC) No 3599/82 of 21 December 1982 on temporary importation arrangements (13)[90], as last amended by Regulation (EEC) No 1620/85 (14)[91];
- Council Regulation (EEC) No 2763/83 of 26 September 1983 on arrangements permitting goods to be processed under customs control before being put into free circulation (15)[92], as last amended by Regulation (EEC) No 720/91(16)[93];
- Council Regulation (EEC) No 2151/84 of 23 July 1984 on the customs territory of the Community (17)[94], as last amended by the Act of Accession of Spain and Portugal;
- Council Regulation (EEC) No 1999/85 of 16 July 1985 on inward processing relief arrangements (18)[95];
- Council Regulation (EEC) No 3632/85 of 12 December 1985 defining the conditions under which a person may be permitted to make a customs declaration (19)[96];
- Council Regulation (EEC) No 2473/86 of 24 July 1986 on outward processing relief arrangements and the standard exchange system (20)[97];

---

84) OJ No L 205, 13.8.1979, p. 19.
85) OJ No L 281, 12.10.1990, p. 28.
86) OJ No L 134, 31.5.1980, p. 1.
87) OJ No L 388, 30.12.1989, p. 24
88) OJ No L 83, 30.3.1981, p. 40.
89) OJ No L 186, 30.6.1989, p. 1.
90) OJ No L 376, 31.12.1982, p. 1.
91) OJ No L 155, 14.6.1985, p. 54.
92) OJ No L 272, 5.10.1985, p. 1.
93) OJ No L 78, 26.3.1991, p. 9.
94) OJ No L 197, 27.7.1984, p. 1.
95) OJ No L 188, 20.7.1985, p. 1.
96) OJ No L 350, 27.12.1985, p. 1.

- Council Regulation (EEC) No 2144/87 of 13 July 1987 on customs
▼B
debt (1)[98], as last amended by Regulation (EEC) No 4108/88 (2)[99];
- Council Regulation (EEC) No 1031/88 of 18 April 1988 determining the persons liable for payment of a customs debt (3)[100], as last amended by Regulation (EEC) No 1716/90 (4)[101];
- Council Regulation (EEC) No 1970/88 of 30 June 1988 concerning triangular traffic under the outward processing relief arrangements and the standard exchange system (5)[102];
- Council Regulation (EEC) No 2503/88 of 25 July 1988 on customs warehouses (6)[103], as amended by Regulation (EEC) No 2561/90 (7)[104];
- Council Regulation (EEC) No 2504/88 of 25 July 1988 on freezones and free ware-houses (8)[105], as amended by Regulation (EEC) No 1604/92 (9)[106];
- Council Regulation (EEC) No 4151/88 of 21 December 1988 laying down the provisions applicable to goods brought into the customs territory of the Community (10)[107];
- Council Regulation (EEC) No 1854/89 of 14 June 1989 on the entry in the accounts and terms of payment of the amounts of the import duties or export duties resulting from a customs debt (11)[108];
- Council Regulation (EEC) No 1855/89 of 14 June 1989 on the temporary importation of means of transport (12)[109];
- Council Regulation (EEC) No 3312/89 of 30 October 1989 on the temporary importation

---

97) OJ No L 212, 2.8.1986, p. 1.
98) OJ No L 201, 22.7.1987, p. 15.
99) OJ No L 361, 29.12.1988, p. 2.
100) OJ No L 102, 21.4.1988, p. 5.
101) OJ No L 160, 26.6.1990, p. 6.
102) OJ No L 174, 6.7.1988, p. 1.
103) OJ No L 225, 15.8.1988, p. 1.
104) OJ No L 246, 10.9.1990, p. 1.
105) OJ No L 225, 15.8.1988, p. 8.
106) OJ No L 173, 26.6.1992, p. 30.
107) OJ No L 367, 31.12.1988, p. 1.
108) OJ No L 186, 30.6.1989, p. 1.
109) OJ No L 186, 30.6.1989, p. 8.

of containers (13)[110];

? Council Regulation (EEC) No 4046/89 of 21 December 1989 on the security to be given to ensure payment of a customs debt (14)[111];

? Council Regulation (EEC) No 1715/90 of 20 June 1990 on the information provided by the customs authorities of the Member States concerning the classification of goods in the customs nomenclature (15)[112];

- Council Regulation (EEC) No 2726/90 of 17 September 1990 on Community transit (16)[113] ?M1 _____ ?,

- Council Regulation (EEC) No 717/91 of 21 March 1991 concerning he Single Administrative Document (17)[114];

- Council Regulation (EEC) No 719/91 of 21 March 1991 on the use in the Community of TIR carnets and ATA carnets as transit documents (18)[115].

2. In all Community acts where reference is made to the Regulations or Directives referred to in paragraph 1, that reference shall be deemed to refer to this Code.

▼B

Article 252

1. Articles 141, 142 and 143 of Council Regulation (EEC) No 918/83 (1)[116] are hereby repealed.

2. Council Regulation (EEC) No 2658/87 (2)[117], as last amended by Regulation (EEC) No 3492/91 (3)[118], is hereby amended as follows:

   (a) Article 8 is hereby amended as follows: The following words shall be inserted after the word "committee": "provided for in Article 247 of the Community Customs Code".

---

110) OJ No L 321, 4.11.1989, p. 5.
111) OJ No L 388, 30.12.1989, p. 1.
112) OJ No L 388, 30.12.1989, p. 1.
113) OJ No L 262, 26.9.1990, p. 1.
114) OJ No L 78, 26.3.1991, p. 1
115) OJ No L 78, 26.3.1991, p. 6.
116) OJ No L 105, 23.4.1983, p. 1
117) OJ No L 256, 7.9.1987, p. 1.
118) OJ No L 328, 30.11.1991, p. 80.

(b) The introductory sentence in Article 10 (1) is hereby amended as follows: "The representative of the Commission shall submit to the committee provided for in Article 247 of the Community Customs Code a draft…".

(c) Articles 7 and 11 are hereby repealed.'

Article 253

This Regulation shall enter into force on the third day following that of its publication in the Official Journal of the European Communities. It shall apply from 1 January 1994. Title VIII shall not apply to the United Kingdom until 1 January 1995. However, Article 161 and, in so far as they concern re-exportation, Articles 182 and 183 shall apply from 1 January 1993. In so far as the said Articles make reference to provisions in this Code and until such time as such provisions enter into force, the references shall be deemed to allude to th e corresponding provisions in the Regulations and Directives listed in Article 251. Before 1 October 1993, the Council shall, on the basis of a Commission progress report on discussions regarding the consequences to be drawn from the monetary conversion rate used for the application of common agricultural policy measures, review the problem of trade in goods between the Member States in the context of the internal market. This report shall be accompanied by Commission proposals if any, on which the Council shall take a decision in accordance with the provisions of the Treaty. Before 1 January 1998, the Council shall, on the basis of a Commission report, review this Code with a view to making such adaptations as may appear necessary taking into account in particular the achievement of the internal market. This report shall be accompanied by proposals, if any, on which the Council shall take a decision in accordance with the provisions of the Treaty.

부록 Ⅳ. SAD 서식

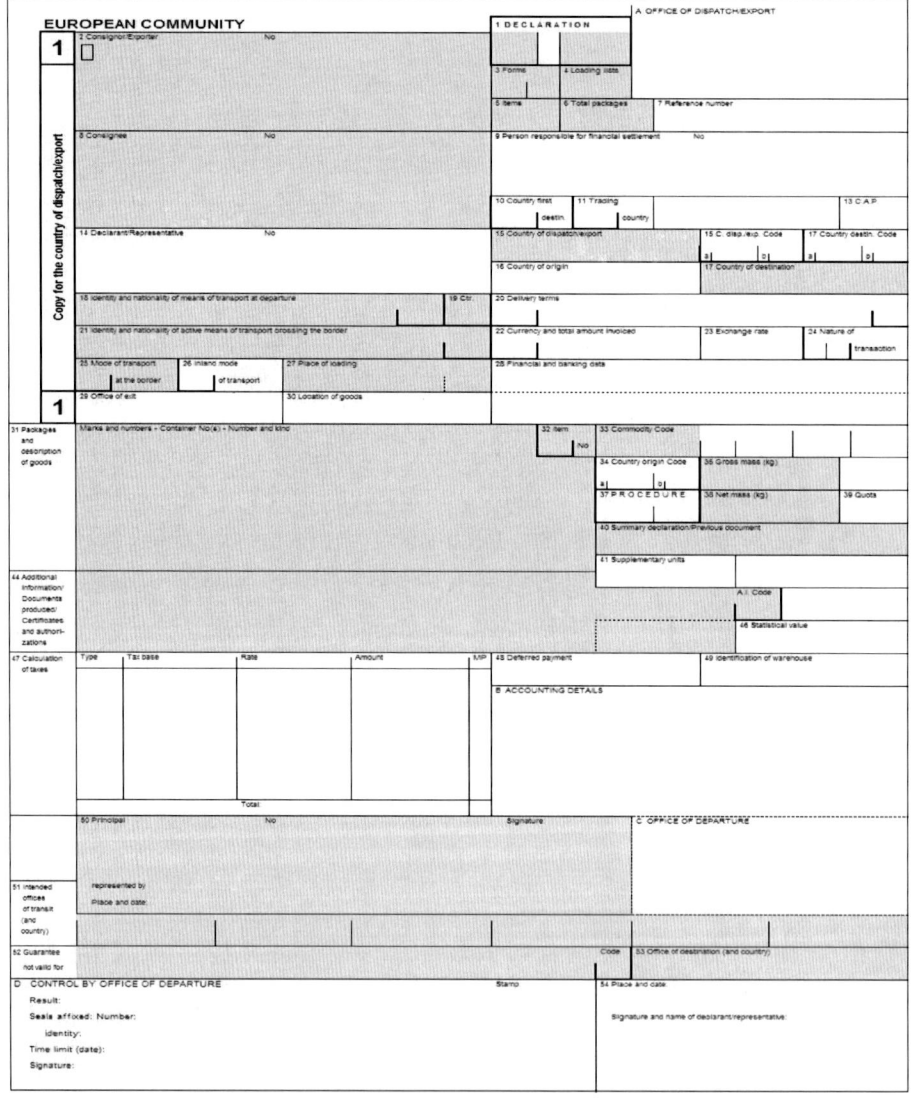

부록 V. EURO 1 Movement Certificate 서식

	MOVEMENT CERTIFICATE	
1. Exporter (Name, full address, country)	**EUR.1 No A 000.000**	
	See notes overleaf before completing this form.	
	2. Certificate used in preferential trade between .... and .... (Insert appropriate countries, groups of countries or territories)	
3. Consignee (Name, full address, country) (Optional)		
	4. Country, group of countries or territory in which the products are considered as originating	5. Country, group of countries or territory of destination
6. Transport details (Optional)	7. Remarks	
8. Item number; Marks and numbers; Number and kind of packages ([1]); Description of goods	9. Gross mass (kg) or other measure (litres, m³, etc.)	10. Invoices (Optional)

11. CUSTOMS ENDORSEMENT	12. DECLARATION BY THE EXPORTER
Declaration certified Export document ([2]) Form .... No .... Of .... Customs office .... Issuing country or territory .... (Place and date) .... (Signature) *Stamp*	I, the undersigned, declare that the goods described above meet the conditions required for the issue of this certificate. .... (Place and date) .... (Signature)

([1]) If goods are not packed, indicate number of articles or state 'in bulk' as appropriate.
([2]) Complete only where the regulations of the exporting country or territory require.

13. REQUEST FOR VERIFICATION, to	14. RESULT OF VERIFICATION
Verification of the authenticity and accuracy of this certificate is requested. .... (Place and date) .... (Signature) *Stamp*	Verification carried out shows that this certificate ([1]) ☐ was issued by the customs office indicated and that the information contained there in is accurate. ☐ does not meet the requirements as to authenticity and accuracy (see remarks appended). .... (Place and date) .... (Signature) *Stamp*

([1]) Insert X in the appropriate box.

부록 VI. IE599 메세지 형식(세관발행 수출가능 메시지)

Export confirmation (IE599) LRN

Email address
Declaration by
Customs inspection results export   Term of exit   exit   Dates declaration   IE515 LRN: MRN: , release   , exit

Summary

Sender		TIN	EORI	Type of IE515 document
				customs office export exit
Consignee				No of line items
				No of packages
Declarant representation type representative		TIN	REGON	Gross weight
Date				Country of dispatch
				Country of destination
			Customs agent license no	CRN:
Transport at border				Incoterms: code
Place of goods customs office				Transaction type value exchange rate
				Seals: number markings

Goods

No	Tariff codes	Goods description	Statistical value	Documents	Other
				Attached documents	Net weight
					Procedure
					Goods amount
					Packages amount markings
					Additional costs code: amount:
				Additional information	